ANARCHY in ACTION

ANARCHY
in ACTION

Colin Ward

LONDON
FREEDOM PRESS

First published
1973
by George Allen & Unwin Ltd
This edition, with a new introduction,
published by Freedom Press
84b Whitechapel High Street
London E1 7QX
1982, reprinted in 1996, 2001

ISBN 0 900384 20 4

In Memory of
PAUL GOODMAN
1911 – 1972

printed in Great Britain by Aldgate Press
Unit 6, Gunthorpe Street Workshops, Gunthorpe Street, London, E1

CONTENTS

INTRODUCTION TO THE SECOND EDITION

The anarchist movement grows in times of popular self-activity, feeds it and feeds off it, and declines when that self-activity declines…The anarchists in England have paid for the gap between their day-to-day activities and their utopian aspirations. This gap consists basically of a lack of strategy, a lack of ability to assess the general situation and initiate a general project which is consistent with the anarchist utopia, and which is not only consistent with anarchist tactics but inspires them.

JOHN QUAIL, *The Slow Burning Fuse:*
The Lost History of the British Anarchists (Paladin 1978)

Anarchism as a political and social ideology has two separate origins. It can be seen as an ultimate derivative of liberalism or as a final end for socialism. In either case, the problems that face the anarchist propagandist are the same. The ideas he is putting forward are so much at variance with ordinary political assumptions, and the solutions he offers are so remote, there is such a gap between what *is*, and what, according to the anarchist, *might be*, that his audience cannot take him seriously.

One elementary principle of attempting to teach anyone anything is that you attempt to build on the common foundation of common experience and common knowledge. That is the intention of the present volume.

This book was commissioned by the publishers Allen and Unwin and originally appeared from them in 1973, and was subsequently published in America and, in translation, in Dutch, Italian, Spanish and Japanese. It was not intended for people who had spent a life-time pondering the problems of anarchism, but for those who either had no idea of what the word implied, or who knew exactly what it implied, and had rejected it, considering that it had no relevance for the modern world.

My original preference as a title was the more cumbersome but more accurate 'Anarchism as a theory of organisation', because as I urge in my preface, that is what the book is about. It is not about strategies for

7

revolution and it is not involved with speculation on the way an anarchist society would function. It is about the ways in which people organise *themselves* in any kind of human society, whether we care to categorise those societies as primitive, traditional, capitalist or communist.

In this sense the book is simply an extended, updating footnote to Kropotkin's *Mutual Aid*. Since it was written I have edited for a modern readership two other works of his, and I am bound to say that the experience has enhanced my agreement with George Orwell's conclusion that Peter Kropotkin was 'one of the most persuasive of anarchist writers' because of his 'inventive and pragmatic outlook'.

In particular, as an amplification of some of the ideas expressed in the present volume, I would like readers to be aware of the edition I prepared of his *Fields, Factories and Workshops* (London: 1974, reprinted with additional material by Freedom Press, 1985) New York: Harper & Row 1975, Milan: Edizioni Antistato 1975, Stockholm: Wahlstrom & Widstrand 1980). Anyone who wants to understand the real nature of the crisis of the British economy in the nineteen-eighties would gain more enlightenment from Kropotkin's analysis from the eighteen-nineties than from the current spokesmen of any of the political parties.

But if this book is just a footnote to Kropotkin, and if it is open to the same criticism as his book (that it is a selective gathering of anecdotal evidence to support the points that the author wants to make) it does attempt to look at a variety of aspects of daily life in the light of traditional anarchist contentions about the nature of authority and the propensity for self-organisation.

Many years of attempting to be an anarchist propagandist have convinced me that we win over our fellow citizens to anarchist ideas, precisely through drawing upon the common experience of the informal, transient, self-organising networks of relationships that in fact make the human community possible, rather than through the rejection of existing society as a whole in favour of some future society where some different kind of humanity will live in perfect harmony.

Since this edition is a reproduction of the original text, my purpose here is to add a few comments and further references, both to update it and to take note of critical comments.

ANARCHY AND THE STATE (pp 21-30)

This is a restatement of the classical anarchist criticism of government and the state, emphasising the historical division between anarchism and Marxism. In 1848, the year of the Communist Manifesto, Proudhon gave vent to an utterance of marvellous invective, which I had meant to include in this chapter:

'To be ruled is to be kept an eye on, inspected, spied on, regulated, indoctrinated, sermonised, listed and checked-off, estimated, appraised, censured, ordered about, by creatures without knowledge and without virtues. To be ruled is, at every operation, transaction, movement, to be noted, registered, counted, priced, admonished, prevented, reformed, redressed, corrected. It is, on the pretext of public utility and in the name of the common good, to be put under contribution, exercised, held to ransom, exploited, monopolised, concussed, pressured, mystified, robbed; then, at the least resistance and at the first hint of complaint, repressed, fined, vilified, vexed, hunted, exasperated, knocked-down, disarmed, garroted, imprisoned, shot, grape-shot, judged, condemned, deported, sacrificed, sold, tricked; and to finish off with, hoaxed, calumniated, dishonoured. Such is government! And to think that there are democrats among us who claim there's some good in government!'

That must have seemed a ludicrous over-statement in 19th-century France. But wouldn't it be perfectly comprehensible to any citizen who steps out of line in any of the totalitarian regimes of the Right or Left that today govern the greater part of the world? Among the attributes of government which Proudhon did not include in his list of horrors, is systematic torture, a unique prerogative of governments in the 20th century.

When this chapter was previously published in a symposium on Participatory Democracy the editors made comments which I found both gratifying and suggestive of ways in which its thesis could be extended. They wrote:

'The anarchist critique of the state, which has often seemed simplistic, is here presented in one of its most sophisticated forms. Here the state is conceived of as the formalisation – and rigidification – of the unused power that the social order has abdicated. In American society it takes the form of a coalition of political, military, and industrial elites, pre-empting space that is simply not occupied by the rest of society.

'Ward believes that the state represents a kind of relationship between people which becomes formalised into a set of vested interests that operates contrary to the interests of the people – even to the point where it evaluates its means in terms of megadeaths. One could take the number of people employed directly by the state as a function of total populations, the amount of state spending as a function of total spending (in socialist states this would require careful functional definition of what constituted the domain of the state as opposed to the social order) and in general compare the resource use of the two areas. One could then analyse the social order in terms of degree of participation, key decisions involving utilisation of social resources and who makes them. Studies of the correlations between state power and social participation in various countries would verify Ward's thesis: those countries that are top-heavy with state power are the countries in which social participation is weak. A more devastating critique of statism could probably not be imagined.'

THE THEORY OF SPONTANEOUS ORDER (pp 31-39)

This chapter drew largely on popular experience of revolutionary situations, actual or potential, before a New Order had filled the gap occupied by the old order. In addition to the works cited on p. 146, several more studies of the Spanish revolution of 1936 have become available since, notably the English translation of Gaston Leval's *Collectives in the Spanish Revolution* (Freedom Press 1975).

To the experience of Hungary in 1956 and Czechoslovakia in 1968 must be added that of Poland in 1980. However the story ends, the achievements of Solidarity in forcing concessions, without loss of life, on a ruling bureaucracy which had not hesitated a decade earlier to order its forces to shoot down striking workers, is a remarkable triumph of working-class self organisation.

THE DISSOLUTION OF LEADERSHIP (pp 40-44)
HARMONY THROUGH COMPLEXITY (pp 45–52)
TOPLESS FEDERATIONS (pp 53-58)

These three chapters, using non-anarchist sources, try to set out three key principles of an anarchist theory of organisation: the concept of leaderless groups, the notion that a healthy society *needs* diversity rather than unity, and the idea of federalist organisations without a central authority. A number of more recent books reinforce the evidence for these chapters. Proudhon's *Du Principe Federatif* has at last been published in English. (Translated by Richard Vernon, University of Toronto Press 1979) The inferences drawn from the history of Swiss federalism are enhanced by Jonathan Steinberg's *Why Switzerland?* (Cambridge University Press 1976), and the anthropological material on stateless societies is added to in part five of Kirkpatrick Sale's *Human Scale* (Secker & Warburg 1980).

WHO IS TO PLAN? (pp 59-66) WE HOUSE, YOU ARE HOUSED, THEY ARE HOMELESS (pp 67-73)

The arguments of these two chapters are set out at much greater length in my books *Tenants Take Over* (Architectural Press 1974) and *Talking Houses* (Freedom Press 1990) as well as in John Turner's *Housing by People* (Marion Boyars 1976).

OPEN AND CLOSED FAMILIES (pp 74-78)

One reviewer criticised this chapter for its claim that the revolution in sexual behaviour in our own day is an essentially anarchist revolution, because in his view it was simply a result of a chemico-technical break-through, the contraceptive pill. My own Dutch translator felt that it was marred by an absence of appreciation of the feminist point of view. I don't think so myself, but I do think that this chapter just skates over the surface of the dilemmas of personal freedom and parental responsibility. As Sheila Rowbotham wrote recently, 'A campaign for child care which demands both the liberation of women and the liberation of children not only reveals the immediate tensions between the two; it also requires a society based on cooperation and free association.'

SCHOOLS NO LONGER (pp 79-86)

This chapter needs no updating, but is extended to some degree by a lecture of mine called 'Towards a Poor School', published in *Talking Schools,* (Freedom Press, 1995) as well as by Chapter 16 of my book *The Child in the City.* Of the various occupations in which I worked for forty years, teaching is the only one which I have a government licence to perform. I am the author of several school books, and the former director of a Schools Council project. I am even a former branch secretary of one of the teaching unions. Yet on every significant issue I have found myself totally opposed to the views of the teaching profession. It sought, and won, the raising of the minimum age limit for compulsory schooling. I favoured its abolition. It wants to eliminate the 'private sector' in education, while I see it as the one guarantee that genuine radical experiment can happen. It *opposes* the abandonment of the legal right to hit children.

I am well aware that the organised opinion of the profession is not the same as that of individual teachers. I revere education. I just can't stomach the dreadful pretensions of the education industry, especially when compared with the results. And I know that my misgivings about education are paralleled by a consideration of any other aspect of the contemporary West-European corporate state, like, for example, the health service or the public provision of housing.

None of my own writings, alas, can be said to propound an anarchist theory of education, but they do raise some of the ironies and paradoxes of attempts to achieve economic equality or social change through the manipulation of the education system. A brave effort to draw together the various streams of anarchist ideas on education is made in Joel H. Spring's *A Primer of Libertarian Education* (New York: Free Life Editions, 1975).

PLAY AS AN ANARCHIST PARABLE (pp 87-93)

Play *is* a parable of anarchy, since it is an area of human activity which is self-chosen and self-directed, but this very fact leads to a comparison with work.

WORK IS	LEISURE IS
Hated	Enjoyed
Long	Brief
For someone else	For yourself
Essential for livelihood	Inessential for livelihood
Concentrated	At your own pace
For fixed hours	In your own time

I quote this polarisation from my school book on *Work* (Penguin Education 1972), because any discussion of play and of leisure (Britain's fastest-growing industry') leads to a consideration of what is wrong with people's working lives.

A SELF-EMPLOYED SOCIETY (pp 94-106)

This is the chapter which is most in need of bringing up to date, but which has an enormously relevant title. Readers do need reminding that for several decades, until the 1960s, the anarchists (apart from a few faithful stalwarts of the producer co-operative movement) were virtually the only people publishing propaganda for worker self-management in industry. Since this book was first published there have been a variety of new experiences and new ventures, and an absolute mountain of new literature.

In left-wing political circles in Britain, for sixty years, the demand for workers' self-management was regarded as a marginal and diversionary issue compared with the demand for nationalisation, the universal cure-all. The atmosphere changed only in the 1970s, when, as an alternative to quiet extinction, workers in a number of enterprises threatened by closure, sought, through protracted 'sit-ins' to demand that they should be helped to keep the plant open under workers' control. Readers will remember the particular local epics at Upper Clyde Shipbuilders at Govan, at the former Fisher-Bendix factory outside Liverpool, at the Scottish Daily Express, at Fakenham Enterprises in Norfolk and at the Meriden motorcycle plant at Coventry.

When Anthony Wedgwood Benn persuaded his fellow members of the Labour government to back these aspirations with public money (a policy which would have been followed automatically when ordinary capitalist industry was concerned), it represented a complete turn-around in his interpretation of socialism as applied to industry. For it was Mr Benn who, in the 1964 Labour government, had been the master-mind, through his Industrial Reorganisation Corporation, of the take-over of half the motor industry by Leylands (a formerly successful bus and lorry firm from Lancashire) and most of the electrical industry by GEC, in the hope of enabling British industry to compete on equal terms for the continental market with the European giants.

These were vain hopes, and one of the glumly hilarious spectacles of the 1980s has been to see a Conservative government, committed to laissez-faire liberalism, continually bailing out British Leyland from tax revenue. The Benn-sponsored co-ops have mostly collapsed, or have had to rely so completely on capitalist investment that their co-operative structure has been submerged. It was only because these firms were dying that the workers' aspirations were given an airing, and there are even people with a conspiratorial view of history who see the whole episode as having been invented to discredit the co-operative ideal.

But as unemployment continually increases in Britain, people who have lost confidence in the usual political panaceas, have shown an increasing interest in co-operative ventures. The British discovered the Mondragon co-operatives in the Basque country, with pilgrimages of trade union officers and local councillors going to Spain to discover the secret of Mondragon's success. The significant recent books are *Worker-Owners: The Mondragon Achievement* (Anglo-German Foundation 1977), Robert Oakeshott's *The Case for Workers' Co-ops* (Routledge & Kegan Paul 1978), *Workers' Co-operatives: A Handbook* (Aberdeen People's Press 1980) and Jenny Thornley: *Workers' Co-operatives: Jobs and Dreams* (Heinemann 1981).

The majority of recent co-operative ventures cannot be regarded as success stories: they have failed. Nor are the apparent pre-conditions for success particularly acceptable to anarchists. Robert Oakeshott, for example, concludes that there are at least four such conditions: 'first, the main thrust to get the enterprises off the ground must come from the potential workforce itself; second, the commitment of the workforce needs to be further secured by the requirement of a meaningful capital stake; third, the prospective enterprise must be equipped with a manager or a management team which is at least not inferior to that which a conventional enterprise would enjoy; fourth, these enterprises must work together in materially supportive groupings, for in isolation they are hopelessly vulnerable.'

THE BREAKDOWN OF WELFARE (pp 107-121)

This chapter does have the merit of raising issues which are unfashion-able both among the defenders of the contemporary British welfare state and among its critics. Since it was written we have moved into the era of cuts in welfare expenditure, imposed by both Labour and Conservative governments. It is not at all easy to take part in the arguments surrounding the cuts from an anarchist point of view. On the one hand we have the political left which regards the provision of welfare, subsidised housing or subsidised transport as a 'social wage' which mitigates the exploitation which it associates with the capitalist system. On the other hand is the political right which claims that the people who derive most from the public services are people who could perfectly well afford to meet their true cost. (And in fact it is perfectly true that the poor derive the least from welfare provision). The whole argument is complicated by the fact that we have now entered the period of mass unemployment.

Welfare is administered by a top-heavy governmental machine which ensures that when economies in public expenditure are imposed by its political masters, they are made by reducing the service to the public, not by reducing the cost of administration. Thus, as Leslie Chapman remarked in his book *Your Disobedient Servant*, in this way 'the wicked injustice of the cuts, the desirability of replacing them as quickly as possible, the unwisdom of those who imposed them and the long suffering patience of those who received them were all demonstrated in one convenient package.' This was subsequently demonstrated during both Labour and Conservative governments. Writing in 1977, A. H. Halsey observed that 'we live today under sentence of death by a thousand cuts, that is, of all things except the body of bureaucracy'. And Peter Townsend noted two years later commenting on 'Social Policy in Conditions of Scarcity' that 'services to consumers or clients were much more vulnerable than staff establishments.'

This was nowhere better demonstrated than in the evolution of the National Health Service. In the ten years before its reorganisation, health service staff generally increased by 65 per cent. However, during that period medical and nursing staff increased by only 21 per cent and domestic staff by 2 per cent. The rest was administration. The government hired a firm of consultants, McKinsey's, to advise on reorganisation. The members of McKinsey's staff who produced the new structure are now convinced that they gave the wrong advice. Similarly the former chief architect to the DHSS is now convinced that the advice he gave for ten years on hospital design was in fact misguided.

We have failed to come to terms with the fact that our publicly-provided services, just like our capitalist industries, also propped up by taxation, are dearly bought. This was less apparent in the past when public services were few and cheap. Old people who recall the marvellous service they used to get from the post office or the railways, never mention that these used to be low wage industries which, in return for relative security, were run with a military-style discipline, to which not even the army, let alone you or I, would submit today.

Any public service nowadays has to pay the going rate, and there is every reason why this should be so. The question at issue is whether government provision is the best way of meeting social needs. We are always offering superior advice to those third world countries where 'aid' is dissipated in the cost of administering it, but we are in just the same situation ourselves. 'Added to the traditional burdens of the poor,' remark the authors of *The Wincroft Youth Project*, 'there is now the weight of a bureaucracy that, ironically, is employed to serve them.'

HOW DEVIANT DARE YOU GET? (pp 122-129)

This chapter deals, however inadequately, with the objection most people raise to anarchist ideas: the anarchist rejection of the law, the legal system and the agencies of law-enforcement. Since this book was first published there have been three new contributions to this debate. One, which, sadly, fails to live up to the promise of its title is Larry Tifft and Dennis Sullivan: *The Struggle to be Human: Crime, Criminology and Anarchism* (Cienfuegos Press 1980). Another is Alan Ritter's *Anarchism: A Theoretical Analysis* (Cambridge University Press 1980) whose author concludes on this issue that 'Even under anarchy there remains some danger of misconduct, which authority sanctioned by rebuke prevents. Though anarchists do not call this rebuke punishment, it is easy to show that they should.' The third, and most suggestive is the chapter on 'A Policy for Crime Control' in Stuart Henry's *The Hidden Economy* (Martin Robertson 1978). Henry argues for what he calls normative control of crime, by which he means 'group or community control'. He remarks that, 'It may be too early to predict, but it would seem that the administration of criminal justice for some types of offence may be about to complete a full circle. Beginning with community control in an underdeveloped society, we have progressed through various stages of formal, professional, bureaucratic justice as industrialisation has gathered momentum. However, recent years have witnessed a new wave of dissatisfaction with centralised, bureaucratic structures through which most aspects of our life are managed. In areas as diverse as government, industry, health and welfare, the emerging trend is towards devolution, decentralisation, democratisation and popular participation. A part of this trend is the de-centralisation of criminal justice to a form of community control which was once commonplace ... Many commentators are rapidly reaching the conclusion that only people involved in and aware of the community can act as effective forces in crime prevention and that simply increasing police and court capacity will neither solve the problems presently plaguing criminal justice systems, nor equip these systems to cope with changing trends in crime. It is felt that the only way out of the present situation is for criminal justice and the community to be brought closer together, so that those who judge and those who are judged are part of the same society ... I believe that only with this degree of involvement and understanding can we ever hope to liberate ourselves from the hypocrisy of our attitude to 'crime', and only then will we be capable of controlling it.'

ANARCHY AND A PLAUSIBLE FUTURE (pp 130-137)

The muted and tentative conclusions of this chapter still seem to me to be valid. If I were writing it today I would certainly have had more to say about the collapse of employment. When this book was written Britain had 800,000 workers registered as unemployed. This was thought at the time to be a scandalous and totally unacceptable figure. Eight years later the figure has risen to 3 million (October 1981). Belatedly we are groping after alternative forms of work to employment. Nobody really believes that manufacturing industry is going to recover lost markets. Nobody really believes that robots or microprocessors are going to create more than a small proportion of the jobs they displace. Finally we have even lost faith in the idea that the service economy is going to expand to fill the jobs lost in the production economy. Jonathan Gershuny shows in his book *After Industrial Society* (Macmillan 1979) that service industries themselves are already declining and that what is more likely to emerge is a *self-service* economy.

It is the inexorable whittling away of employment that is leading to speculation about the potential of other ways of organising work, a theme of several chapters in this book. The pre-industrial economy was a domestic economy, (Elliot Jacques reminds us that the word 'employment' has only been used in its present sense since the 1840s), and perhaps a domestic economy of individual or collective self-employment is the pattern for the future of work. Hence the growing interest in what is variously termed the irregular economy, the informal economy, or the black economy. Gershuny and Ray Pahl invite us to consider a future in which more and more people move out of 'employment' into working for themselves. 'Is it sapping the moral fibre of the nation or is it strengthening kin links and neighbourly relations more than armies of social workers and priests have ever been able to do? What, in a phrase, will it be like to live in a world dominated more and more by household and hidden economies and less by the formal economy?'

One of the possibilities they see is of a dual labour market: a high-pay, high technology, aristocracy of labour and a low-wage, low-skill sector, and beyond both the mafiosi of big bosses and little crooks. Another is of a police state dominated by a vast bureaucracy of law enforcement, where 'people would feel much like those caught in the "socialism" of Poland or Czechoslovakia.'

Their third, and more hopeful, alternative depends on 'a deeper understanding of the socially desirable aspects of the informal economy and by sympathetic encouragement of them.' But who is going to give sympathetic encouragement to the dismantling of industrialism, one of the bulwarks of social control? Not the captains of industry. Not the manipulators of the machinery of government.

Suppose our future in fact lies, not with a handful of technocrats pushing buttons to support the rest of us, but with a multitude of small activities, whether by individuals or groups, doing their own thing? Suppose the only plausible economic recovery consists in people picking themselves up off the industrial scrapheap, or rejecting their slot in the micro-technology system, and making their own niche in the world of ordinary needs and their satisfaction. Wouldn't that be something to do with anarchism?

1981   **C. W.**

PREFACE

'Nothing to declare?' 'Nothing.' Very well. Then political questions. He asks: 'Are you an anarchist ?' I answer. ' ... First, what do we understand under "anarchism"? Anarchism practical, metaphysical, theoretical, mystical, abstractional, individual, social? When I was young', I say, 'all these had for me signification.' So we had a very interesting discussion, in consequence of which I passed two whole weeks on Ellis Island.

VLADIMIR NABOKOV, *Pnin*

How would you feel if you discovered that the society in which you would really like to live was already here, apart from a few little, local difficulties like exploitation, war, dictatorship and starvation? The argument of this book is that an anarchist society, a society which organises itself without authority, is always in existence, like a seed beneath the snow, buried under the weight of the state and its bureaucracy, capitalism and its waste, privilege and its injustices, nationalism and its suicidal loyalties, religious differences and their superstitious separatism.

Of the many possible interpretations of anarchism the one presented here suggests that, far from being a speculative vision of a future society, it is a description of a mode of human organisation, rooted in the experience of everyday life, which operates side by side with, and in spite of, the dominant authoritarian trends of our society. This is not a new version of anarchism. Gustav Landauer saw it, not as the founding of something new, 'but as the actualisation and reconstitution of something that has always been present, which exists alongside the state, albeit buried and laid waste'. And a modern anarchist, Paul Goodman, declared that: 'A free society cannot be the substitution of a "new order" for the old order; it is the extension of spheres of free action until they make up most of social life.'

You may think that in describing anarchy as *organisation*, I am being deliberately paradoxical. Anarchy you may consider to be, by definition, the *opposite* of organisation. But the word really means something quite

18

different; it means the absence of government, the absence of authority. It is, after all, governments which make and enforce the laws that enable the 'haves' to retain control of social assets to the exclusion of the 'have-nots'. It is, after all, the principle of authority which ensures that people will work for someone else for the greater part of their lives, not because they enjoy it or have any control over their work, but because to do so is their only means of livelihood. It is, after all, governments which prepare for and wage war, even though *you* are obliged to suffer the consequences of their going to war.

But is it only governments? The power of a government, even the most absolute dictatorship, depends on the agreement of the governed. Why do people consent to be ruled? It isn't only fear; what have millions of people to fear from a small group of professional politicians and their paid strong-arm men? It is because they subscribe to the same values as their governors. Rulers and ruled alike believe in the principle of authority, of hierarchy, of power. They even feel themselves privileged when, as happens in a small part of the globe, they can choose between alternative labels on the ruling elites. And yet, in their ordinary lives they keep society going by voluntary association and mutual aid.

Anarchists are people who make a social and political philosophy out of the natural and spontaneous tendency of humans to associate together for their mutual benefit. Anarchism is in fact the name given to the idea that it is possible and desirable for society to organise itself without government. The word comes from the Greek, meaning *without authority,* and ever since the time of the Greeks there have been advocates of anarchy under one name or another. The first person in modern times to evolve a systematic theory of anarchism was William Godwin, soon after the French revolution. A Frenchman, Proudhon, in the mid-nineteenth century developed an anarchist theory of social organisation, of small units federated together but with no central power. He was followed by the Russian revolutionary, Michael Bakunin, the contemporary and adversary of Karl Marx. Marx represented one wing of the socialist movement, concentrating on seizing the power of the state, Bakunin represented the other, seeking the destruction of state power.

Another Russian, Peter Kropotkin, sought to give a scientific foundation to anarchist ideas by demonstrating that mutual aid – voluntary co-operation – is just as strong a tendency in human life as aggression and the urge to dominate. These famous names of anarchism recur in this book, simply because what they wrote speaks, as the Quakers say, to our condition. But there were thousands of other obscure revolutionaries, propagandists and teachers who never wrote books for me to quote but who tried to spread the idea of society without government in almost every country in the world, and especially in the revolutions in Mexico, Russia and Spain. Everywhere they were defeated, and the historians wrote that anarchism finally died when Franco's troops entered Barcelona in 1939.

But in Paris in 1968 anarchist flags flew over the Sorbonne, and in the same year they were seen in Brussels, Rome, Mexico City, New York, and even in Canterbury. All of a sudden people were talking about the need for the kind of politics in which ordinary men, women and children decide their own fate and make their own future, about the need for social and political decentralisation, about workers' control of industry, about pupil power in school, about community control of the social services. Anarchism, instead of being a romantic historical by-way, becomes an attitude to human organisation which is more relevant today than it ever seemed in the past.

Organisation and its problems have developed a vast and expanding literature because of the importance of the subject for the hierarchy of government administration and industrial management. Very little of this vast literature provides anything of value for the anarchist except in his role as destructive critic or saboteur of the organisations that dominate our lives. The fact is that while there are thousands of students and teachers of government, there are hardly any of non-government. There is an immense amount of research into methods of administration, but hardly any into self-regulation. There are whole libraries on, and expensive courses in, industrial management, and very large fees for consultants in management, but there is scarcely any literature, no course of study and certainly no fees for those who want to do away with management and substitute workers' autonomy. The brains are sold to the big battalions, and we have to build up a theory of non-government, of non-management, from the kind of history and experience which has hardly been written about because nobody thought it all that important.

'History', said W. R. Lethaby, 'is written by those who survive, philosophy by the well-to-do; those who go under have the experience.' But once you begin to look at human society from an anarchist point of view you discover that the alternatives are already there, in the interstices of the dominant power structure. If you want to build a free society, the parts are all at hand.

Chapter I

ANARCHY AND THE STATE

As long as today's problems are stated in terms of mass politics and 'mass organisation', it is clear that only States and mass parties can deal with them. But if the solutions that can be offered by the existing States and parties are acknowledged to be either futile or wicked, or both, then we must look not only for different 'solutions' but especially for a different way of stating the problems themselves.

ANDREA CAFFI

If you look at the history of socialism, reflecting on the melancholy difference between promise and performance, both in those countries where socialist parties have triumphed in the struggle for political power, and in those where they have never attained it, you are bound to ask yourself what went wrong, when and why. Some would see the Russian revolution of 1917 as the fatal turning point in socialist history. Others would look as far back as the February revolution of 1848 in Paris as 'the starting point of the two-fold development of European socialism, anarchistic and Marxist',[1] while many would locate the critical point of divergence as the congress of the International at The Hague in 1872, when the exclusion of Bakunin and the anarchists signified the victory of Marxism. In one of his prophetic criticisms of Marx that year Bakunin previsaged the whole subsequent history of Communist society:

> Marx is an authoritarian and centralising communist. He wants what we want, the complete triumph of economic and social equality, but he wants it in the State and through the State power, through the dictatorship of a very strong and, so to say, despotic provisional government, that is by the negation of liberty. His economic ideal is the State as sole owner of the land and of all kinds of capital, cultivating the land under the management of State engineers, and controlling all industrial and commercial associations with State capital. We want the same triumph

21

of economic and social equality through the abolition of the State and of all that passes by the name of law (which, in our view, is the permanent negation of human rights). We want the reconstruction of society and the unification of mankind to be achieved, not from above downwards by any sort of authority, nor by socialist officials, engineers, and other accredited men of learning – but from below upwards, by the free federation of all kinds of workers' associations liberated from the yoke of the State.[2]

The home-grown English variety of socialism reached the point of divergence later. It was possible for one of the earliest Fabian Tracts to declare in 1886 that 'English Socialism is not yet Anarchist or Collectivist, not yet defined enough in point of policy to be classified. There is a mass of Socialistic feeling not yet conscious of itself as Socialism. But when the unconscious Socialists of England discover their position, they also will probably fall into two parties: a Collectivist party supporting a strong central administration and a counterbalancing Anarchist party defending individual initiative against that administration.'[3] The Fabians rapidly found which side of the watershed was theirs and when a Labour Party was founded they exercised a decisive influence on its policies. At its annual conference in 1918 the Labour Party finally committed itself to that interpretation of socialism which identified it with the unlimited increase of the State's power and activity through its chosen form: the giant managerially-controlled public corporation.

And when socialism has achieved power what has it created? Monopoly capitalism with a veneer of social welfare as a substitute for social justice. The large hopes of the nineteenth century have not been fulfilled; only the gloomy prophecies have come true. The criticism of the state and of the structure of its power and authority made by the classical anarchist thinkers has increased in validity and urgency in the century of total war and the total state, while the faith that the conquest of state power would bring the advent of socialism has been destroyed in every country where socialist parties have won a parliamentary majority, or have ridden to power on the wave of a popular revolution, or have been installed by Soviet tanks. What has happened is exactly what the anarchist Proudhon, over a hundred years ago, said would happen. All that has been achieved is 'a compact democracy having the appearance of being founded on the dictatorship of the masses, but in which the masses have no more power than is necessary to ensure a general serfdom in accordance with the following precepts and principles borrowed from the old absolutism: indivisibility of public power, all-consuming centralisation, systematic destruction of all individual, corporative and regional thought (regarded as disruptive), inquisitorial police.'[4]

Kropotkin, too, warned us that 'The State organisation, having been the force to which the minorities resorted for establishing and organising their power over the masses, cannot be the force which will serve to destroy these privileges,' and he declared that 'the economic and political liberation of man will have to create new forms for its expression in life, instead of those established by the State.'[5] He thought it self-evident that 'this new form will have to be more popular, more decentralised, and nearer to the folk-mote self-government than representative government can ever be,' reiterating that we will be compelled to find new forms of organisation for the social functions that the state fulfils through the bureaucracy, and that 'as long as this is not done, nothing will be done'.[6]

When we look at the *powerlessness* of the individual and the small face-to-face group in the world today and ask ourselves *why* they are powerless, we have to answer not merely that they are weak because of the vast central agglomerations of power in the modern, military-industrial state, but that they are weak *because* they have surrendered their power to the state. It is as though every individual possessed a certain quantity of power, but that by default, negligence, or thoughtless and unimaginative habit or conditioning, he has allowed someone else to pick it up, rather than use it himself for his own purposes. ('According to Kenneth Boulding, there is only so much human energy around. When large organisations utilise these energy resources, they are drained away from the other spheres.')[7]

Gustav Landauer, the German anarchist, made a profound and simple contribution to the analysis of the state and society in one sentence: 'The state is not something which can be destroyed by a revolution, but is a condition, a certain relationship between human beings, a mode of human behaviour; we destroy it by contracting other relationships, by behaving differently.' It is *we* and not an abstract outside identity, Landauer implies, who behave in one way or the other, politically or socially. Landauer's friend and executor, Martin Buber, begins his essay *Society and the State* with an observation of the sociologist, Robert MacIver, that 'to identify the social with the political is to be guilty of the grossest of all confusions, which completely bars any understanding of either society or the state.' The political principle, for Buber, is characterised by power, authority, hierarchy, dominion. He sees the social principle wherever men link themselves in an association based on a common need or common interest.

What is it, Buber asks, that gives the political principle it ascendancy? And he answers, 'the fact that every people feel itself threatened by the others gives the state its definite unifying power; it depends upon the instinct of self-preservation of society itself; the latent external crisis enables it to get the upper hand in internal crises ... All forms of government have this in common: each possesses more power than is required by the given conditions; in fact, this excess in the capacity for making dispositions is actually what we understand by political power. The measure of this excess which cannot, of course, be computed precisely, represents the exact difference between administration and government.' He calls this excess the 'political surplus' and observes that 'its justification derives from the external and internal instability, from the latent state of crisis between nations and within every nation. The political principle is always stronger in relation to the social principle than the given conditions require. The result is a continuous diminution in social spontaneity.'[8]

The conflict between these two principles is a permanent aspect of the human condition. Or as Kropotkin put it: 'Throughout the history of our civilisation, two traditions, two opposed tendencies, have been in conflict: the Roman tradition and the popular tradition, the imperial tradition and the federalist tradition, the authoritarian tradition and the libertarian tradition.' There is an inverse correlation between the two: the strength of one is the weakness of the other. If we want to strengthen society we must weaken the state. Totalitarians of all kinds realise this, which is why they invariably seek to destroy those social institutions which they cannot dominate. So do the dominant interest groups in the state, like the alliance of big business and the military establishment for the 'permanent war economy' suggested by Secretary of Defence Charles E. Wilson in the United States, which has since become so dominant that even Eisenhower, in his last address as President, felt obliged to warn us of its menace.[9]

Shorn of the metaphysics with which politicians and philosophers have enveloped it, the state can be defined as a political mechanism using force, and to the sociologist it is *one* among many forms of social organisation. It is, however, 'distinguished from all other associations by its exclusive investment with the final power of coercion'.[10] And against whom is this final power directed? It is *directed* at the enemy without, but it is *aimed* at the subject society *within*.

This is why Buber declared that it is the maintenance of the latent external crisis that enables the state to get the upper hand in internal crises. Is this a conscious procedure? Is it simply that 'wicked' men control the state, so that we could put things right by voting for 'good' men? Or is it a fundamental characteristic of the state as an institution? It was because she drew this final conclusion that Simone Weil declared that 'The great error of nearly all studies of war, an error into which all socialists have fallen, has been to consider war as an episode in foreign politics, when it is especially an act of interior politics, and the most atrocious act of all.' For just as Marx found that in the era of unrestrained capitalism, competition between employers, knowing no other weapon than the exploitation of their workers, was transformed into a struggle of each employer against his own workmen, and ultimately of the entire employing class against their employees, so the state uses war and the threat of war as a weapon against *its own* population. 'Since the directing apparatus has no other way of fighting the enemy than by sending its own soldiers, under compulsion, to their death – the war of one State against another State resolves itself into a war of the State and the military apparatus against its own people.[11]

It doesn't look like this, of course, if you are a part of the directing apparatus, calculating what proportion of the population you can afford to lose in a nuclear war – just as the governments of all the great powers, capitalist and communist, have calculated. But it does look like this if you are part of the expendable population – unless you identify your own unimportant carcase with the state apparatus – *as millions do*. The expendability factor has increased by being transfered from the specialised, scarce and expensively trained military personnel to the amorphous civilian population. American strategists have calculated the proportion of civilians killed in this century's major wars. In the First World War 5 per cent of those killed were civilians, in the Second World War 48 per cent, in the Korean War 84 per cent, while in a Third World War 90-95 per cent would be civilians. States, great and small, now have a stockpile of nuclear weapons equivalent to ten tons of TNT for every person alive today.

In the nineteenth century T. H. Green remarked that war is the expression of the 'imperfect' state, but he was quite wrong. War is the expression of the state in its most perfect form: it is its finest hour. War is the health of the state – the phrase was invented during the First World War by Randolph Bourne, who explained:

> The State is the organisation of the herd to act offensively or defensively against another herd similarly organised. War sends the current of purpose and activity flowing down to the lowest level of the herd, and to its most remote branches. All the activities of society are linked together as fast as possible to this central purpose of making a military offensive or a military defence, and the State becomes what in peacetime it has vainly struggled to become ... The slack is taken up, the cross-currents fade out, and the nation moves lumberingly and slowly, but with ever accelerated speed and integration, towards the great end, towards that *peacefulness of being at war* ...[12]

This is why the weakening of the state, the progressive development of its imperfections, is a social necessity. The strengthening of *other* loyalties, of *alternative* foci of power, of *different* modes of human behaviour, is an essential for survival. But where do we begin? It ought to be obvious that we do *not* begin by supporting, joining, or hoping to change from within, the existing political parties, nor by starting new ones as rival contenders for political power. Our task is not to gain power, but to erode it, to drain it away from the state. 'The State bureaucracy and centralisation are as irreconcilable with socialism as was autocracy with capitalist rule. One way or another, socialism must become more popular, more communalistic, and less dependent upon indirect government through elected representatives. It must become more self-governing.'[13] Putting it differently, we have to build networks instead of pyramids. All authoritarian institutions are organised as pyramids: the state, the private or public corporation, the army, the police, the church, the university, the hospital: they are all pyramidal structures with a small group of decision-makers at the top and a broad base of people whose decisions are *made for them* at the bottom. Anarchism does not demand the changing of the labels on the layers, it doesn't want different people on top, it wants *us* to clamber out from underneath. It advocates an extended network of individuals and groups, making their own decisions, controlling their own destiny.

The classical anarchist thinkers envisaged the whole social organisation woven from such local groups: the *commune* or council as the territorial nucleus (being 'not a branch of the state, but the free association of the members concerned, which may be either a co-operative or a corporative body, or simply a provisional union of several people united by a common need,'[14]) and the *syndicate* or worker's council as the industrial or occupational unit. These units would federate together not like the stones of a pyramid where the biggest burden is borne by the lowest layer, but like the links of a network, the network of autonomous groups. Several strands of thought are linked together in anarchist social theory: the ideas of direct action, autonomy and workers' control, decenralisation and federalism.

The phrase 'direct action' was first given turrency by the French revolutionary syndicalists of the turn of the century, and was associated with the various forms of militant industrial resistance — the strike, go-slow, working-to-rule, sabotage and the general strike. Its meaning has widened since then to take in the experience of, for example, Gandhi's civil disobedience campaign and the civil rights struggle in the United States, and the many other forms of do-it-yourself politics that are spreading round the world. Direct action has been defined by David Wieck as that 'action which, in respect to a situation, *realises the end desired*, so far as this lies within one's power or the power of one's group' and he distinguishes this from indirect action which realises *an irrelevant or even contradictory* end, presumably as a means to the 'good' end. He gives this as a homely example: 'If the butcher weighs one's meat with his thumb on the scale, one may complain about it and tell him he is a bandit who robs the poor, and if he persists and one does nothing else, this is *mere talk;* one may call the Department of Weights and Measures, and this is *indirect action*; or one may, talk failing, insist on weighing one's own meat, bring along a scale to check the butcher's weight, take one's business somewhere else, help open a co-operative store, and these are *direct actions.*' Wieck observes that: 'Proceeding with the belief that in every situation, every individual and group has the possibility of *some* direct action on *some* level of generality, we may discover much that has been unrecognised, and the importance of much that has been under-rated. So politicalised is our thinking, so focused to the motions of governmental institutions, that the effects of direct efforts to modify one's environment are unexplored. The habit of direct action is, perhaps, identical with the habit of being a free man, prepared to live responsibly in a free society.'[15]

The ideas of autonomy and workers' control and of decentralisation are inseparable from that of direct action. In the modern state, everywhere and in every field, one group of people makes decisions, exercises control, limits choices, while the great majority have to accept these decisions, submit to this control and act within the limits of these externally imposed choices. The habit of direct action is the habit of wresting back the power to make decisions affecting *us* from *them*. The autonomy of the worker at work is the most important field in which this expropriation of decision-making can apply. When workers' control is mentioned, people smile sadly and murmur regretfully that it is a pity that the scale and complexity of modern industry make it a utopian dream which could never be put into practice in a developed economy. They are wrong. There are no *technical* grounds for regarding workers' control as impossible. The obstacles to self-management in industry are the same obstacles that stand in the way of any kind of equitable share-out of society's assets: the vested interest of the privileged in the existing distribution of power and property.

Similarly, decentralisation is not so much a technical problem as an approach to problems of human organisation. A convincing case can be made for decentralisation on economic grounds, but for the anarchist there just isn't any other solution consistent with his advocacy of direct action and autonomy. It doesn't occur to him to seek centralist solutions just as it doesn't occur to the person with an authoritarian and centralising frame of thought to seek decentralist ones. A contemporary anarchist advocate of decentralisation, Paul Goodman, remarks that:

> In fact there have always been two strands to decentralist thinking. Some authors, e.g. Lao-tse or Tolstoy, make a conservative peasant critique of centralised court and town as inorganic, verbal and ritualistic. But other authors, e.g. Proudhon or Kropotkin, make a democratic urban critique of centralised bureaucracy and power, including feudal industrial power, as exploiting, inefficient, and discouraging initiative. In our present era

of State-socialism, corporate feudalism, regimented schooling, brain-washing mass-communications and urban anomie, both kinds of critique make sense. We need to revive both peasant self-reliance and the democratic power of professional and technical guilds.

Any decentralisation that could occur at present would inevitably be post-urban and post-centralist: it could not be provincial ... 16

His conclusion is that decentralisation is 'a kind of social organisation; it does not involve geographical isolation, but a particular sociological use of geography'.

Precisely because we are not concerned with recommending geographical isolation, anarchist thinkers have devoted a great deal of thought to the principle of federalism. Proudhon regarded it as the alpha and omega of his political and economic ideas. He was not thinking of a confederation of states or of a world federal government, but of a basic principle of human organisation.

Bakunin's philosophy of federalism echoed Proudhon's but insisted that only socialism could give it a genuinely revolutionary content, and Kropotkin, too, drew on the history of the French Revolution, the Paris Commune, and, at the very end of his life, the experience of the Russian Revolution, to illustrate the importance of the federal principle if a revolution is to retain its revolutionary content.

Autonomous direct action, decentralised decision-making, and free federation have been the characteristics of all genuinely popular uprisings. Staughton Lynd remarked that 'no real revolution has ever taken place — whether in America in 1776, France in 1789, Russia in 1917, China in 1949 – without *ad hoc* popular institutions improvised from below, simply beginning to administer power in place of the institutions previously recognised as legitimate.' They were seen too in the German uprisings of 1919 like the Munich 'council-republic', in the Spanish Revolution of 1936 and in the Hungarian Revolution of 1956, or in the Spring days in Prague in 1968 – only to be destroyed by the very party which rode to power on the essentially anarchist slogan 'All Power to the Soviets' in 1917. In March 1920, by which time the Bolsheviks had transformed the local soviets into organs of the central administration, Lenin said to Emma Goldman, 'Why, even your great comrade Errico Malatesta has declared himself for the soviets.' 'Yes,' she replied, 'For the *free* soviets.' Malatesta himself, defining the anarchist interpretation of revolution, wrote:

Revolution is the destruction of all coercive ties; it is the autonomy of groups, of communes, of regions, revolution is the free federation brought about by a desire for brotherhood, by individual and collective interests, by the needs of production and defence; revolution is the constitution of innumerable free groupings based on ideas, wishes and tastes of all kinds that exist among the people; revolution is the forming and disbanding of thousands of representative, district, communal, regional, national bodies which, without having any legislative power, serve to make known and to co-ordinate the desires and interests of people near and far and which act through information, advice and example. Revolution is freedom proved in the crucible of facts – and lasts so long as freedom lasts, that is until others, taking advantage of the weariness that overtakes the masses, of the inevitable disappointments that follow exaggerated hopes, of the probable errors and human faults, succeed in constituting a power which, supported by an army of mercenaries or conscripts, lays down the law, arrests the movement at the point it has reached, and then begins the reaction.[17]

His last sentence indicates that he thought reaction inevitable, and so it is, if people are willing to surrender the power they have wrested from a former ruling elite into the hands of a new one. But a reaction to every revolution is inevitable in another sense. This is what the ebb and flow of history implies. The *lutte finale* exists only in the words of a song. As Landauer says, every time after the revolution is a time before the revolution for all those whose lives have not got bogged down in some great moment of the past. There is no final struggle, only a series of partisan struggles on a variety of fronts.

And after over a century of experience of the theory, and over half a century of experience of the practice of the Marxist and social democratic varieties of socialism, after the historians have dismissed anarchism as one of the nineteenth-century also-rans of history, it is emerging again as a coherent social philosophy in the guerilla warfare for a society of participants, which is occurring sporadically all over the world. Thus, commenting on the events of May 1968 in France, Theodore Draper declared that 'The lineage of the new revolutionaries goes back to Bakunin rather than to Marx, and it is just as well that the term "anarchism" is coming back into vogue. For what we have been witnessing is a revival of anarchism in modern dress or masquerading as latter-day Marxism. Just as nineteenth-century Marxism matured in a struggle against anarchism, so twentieth-century Marxism may have to recreate itself in another struggle against anarchism in its latest guise.'[18] He went on to comment that the anarchists did not have much staying-power in the nineteenth century and that it is unlikely that they will have much more in this century. Whether or not he is right about the new anarchists depends on a number of factors. Firstly, on whether or not people have learned *anything* from the history of the last hundred years; secondly, on whether the large number of people in both east and west – the dissatisfied and dissident young of the Soviet empire as well as of the

United States who seek an alternative theory of social organisation – will grasp the relevance of those ideas which we define as anarchism; and thirdly, on whether the anarchists themselves are sufficiently imaginative and inventive to find ways of applying their ideas today to the society we live in in ways that combine immediate aims with ultimate ends.

Chapter II

THE THEORY OF SPONTANEOUS ORDER

In every block of houses, in every street, in every town ward, groups of volunteers will have been organised, and these commissariat volunteers will find it easy to work in unison and keep in touch with each other ... if only the self-styled 'scientific' theorists do not thrust themselves in ... Or rather let them expound their muddle-headed theories as much as they like, provided they have no authority, no power! And that admirable spirit of organisation inherent in the people ... but which they have so seldom been allowed to exercise, will initiate, even in so huge a city as Paris, and in the midst of a revolution, an immense guild of free workers, ready to furnish to each and all the necessary food.

Give the people a free hand, and in ten days the food service will be conducted with admirable regularity. Only those who have never seen the people hard at work, only those who have passed their lives buried among documents, can doubt it. Speak of the organising genius of the 'Great Misunderstood', the people, to those who have seen it in Paris in the days of the barricades, or in London during the great dock strike, when half a million of starving folk had to be fed, and they will tell you how superior it is to the official ineptness of Bumbledom.

PETER KROPOTKIN, *The Conquest of Bread*

An important component of the anarchist approach to organisation is what we might call the theory of spontaneous order: the theory that, given a common need, a collection of people will, by trial and error, by improvisation and experiment, evolve order out of the situation – this order being more durable and more closely related to their needs than any kind of externally imposed authority could provide. Kropotkin derived his version of this theory from his observations of the history of human society as well as from the study of the events of the French Revolution in its early stages and from the Paris Commune of 1871, and it has been witnessed in most revolutionary situations, in the *ad hoc* organisations that spring up after natural disasters, or in any activity

31

where there are no existing organisational forms or hierarchical authority. The principle of authority is so built in to every aspect of our society that it is only in revolutions, emergencies and 'happenings' that the principle of spontaneous order emerges. But it does provide a glimpse of the kind of human behaviour that the anarchist regards as 'normal' and the authoritarian sees as unusual.

You could have seen it in, for example, the first Aldermaston March or in the widespread occupation of army camps by squatters in the summer of 1946, described in Chapter VII. Between June and October of that year 40,000 homeless people in England and Wales, acting on their own initiative, occupied over 1,000 army camps. They organised every kind of communal service in the attempt to make these bleak huts more like home – communal cooking, laundering and nursery facilities, for instance. They also federated into a Squatters' Protection Society. One feature of these squatter communities was that they were formed from people who had very little in common beyond their homelessness – they included tinkers and university dons. It could be seen in spite of commercial exploitation in the pop festivals of the late 1960s, in a way which is not apparent to the reader of newspaper headlines. From 'A cross-section of informed opinion' in an appendix to a report to the government, a local authority representative mentions 'an atmosphere of peace and contentment which seems to be dominant amongst the participants' and a church representative mentions 'a general atmosphere of considerable relaxation, friendliness and a great willingness to share'.[1] The same kind of comments were made about the instant city of the Woodstock Festival in the United States: 'Woodstock, if permanent, would have become one of America's major cities in size alone, and certainly a unique one in the principles by which its citizens conducted themselves.'[2]

An interesting and deliberate example of the theory of spontaneous organisation in operation was provided by the Pioneer Health Centre at Peckham in South London. This was started in the decade before the Second World War by a group of physicians and biologists who wanted to study the nature of health and of healthy behaviour instead of studying ill-health like the rest of the medical profession. They decided that the way to do this was to start a social club whose members joined as families and could use a variety of facilities in return for a family membership subscription and for agreeing to periodic medical examinations. In order to be able to draw valid conclusions the Peckham biologists thought it necessary that they should be able to observe human beings who were free – free to act as they wished and to give expression to their desires. There were consequently no rules, no regulations, no leaders. 'I was the only person with authority,' said Dr Scott Williamson, the founder, 'and I used it to stop anyone exerting any authority.' For the first eight months there was chaos. 'With the first member-families', says one observer, 'there arrived a horde of undisciplined children who used the whole building as they might have used one vast London street. Screaming and running like hooligans through all the rooms, breaking equipment and furniture,' they made life intolerable for everyone. Scott Williamson, however, 'insisted that peace should be restored only by the response of the children to the variety of stimulus that was placed in their way'. This faith was rewarded: 'In less than a year the chaos was reduced to an order in which groups of children could daily be seen swimming, skating, riding bicycles, using the gymnasium or playing some game, occasionally reading a book in the library ... the running and screaming were things of the past.'

In one of the several valuable reports on the Peckham experiment, John Comerford draws the conclusion that 'A society, therefore, if left to itself in suitable circumstances to express itself spontaneously works out its own salvation and achieves a harmony of actions which superimposed leadership cannot emulate.'[3] This is the same inference as was drawn by Edward Allsworth Ross from his study of the true (as opposed to the legendary) evolution of 'frontier' societies in nineteenth-century America.[4]

Equally dramatic examples of the same kind of phenomenon are reported by those people who have been brave enough, or self-confident enough, to institute self-governing, non-punitive communities of 'delinquent' youngsters – August Aichhorn, Homer Lane and David Wills are examples. Homer Lane was the man who, years in advance of his time, started a community of boys and girls, sent to him by the courts, called the Little Commonwealth. He used to declare that 'Freedom cannot be given. It is taken by the child in discovery and invention.' True to this principle, says Howard Jones, 'he refused to impose upon the children a system of government copied from the institutions of the adult world. The self-governing structure of the Little Commonwealth was evolved by the children themselves, slowly and painfully, to satisfy their own needs.'[5] Aichhorn was an equally bold man of the same generation who ran a home for maladjusted children in Vienna. He gives this description of one particularly aggressive group: 'Their aggressive acts became more frequent and more violent until practically all the furniture in the building was destroyed, the window panes broken, the doors nearly kicked to pieces. It happened once that a boy sprang through a double window ignoring his injuries from the broken glass. The dinner table was finally deserted because each one sought out a corner in the playroom where he crouched to devour his food. Screams and howls could be heard from afar!'[6]

Aichhorn and his colleagues maintained what one can only call a superhuman restraint and faith in their method, protecting their charges from the wrath of the neighbours, the police and the city authorities, and 'Eventually patience brought its reward. Not only did the children settle down, but they developed a strong attachment to those who were working with them ... This attachment was now to be used as the foundation of a process of re-education. The children were at last to be brought up against the limitations imposed upon them by the real world.'[7]

Time and again those rare people who have themselves been free enough and have had the moral strength and the endless patience and forbearance that this method demands, have been similarly rewarded. In ordinary life the fact that one is not dealing (theoretically at least,) with such deeply disturbed characters should make the experience less drastic, but in ordinary life, outside the deliberately protected environment, we interact with others with the aim of getting some common task done, and the apparent aimlessness and time-consuming tedium of the period of waiting for spontaneous order to appear brings the danger of some lover of order intervening with an attempt to impose authority and method, just to get something accomplished. But you have only to watch parents with their children to see that the threshold of tolerance for disorder in this context varies enormously from one individual to another. We usually conclude that the punitive, interfering lover of order is usually so because of his own unfreedom and insecurity. The tolerant condoner of disorder is a recognisably different kind of character, and the reader will have no doubt which of the two is easier to live with.

On an altogether different plane is the spontaneous order that emerges in those rare moments in human society when a popular revolution has withdrawn support, and consequently power, from the forces of 'law-and-order'. I once spoke to a Scandinavian journalist back from a visit to South Africa, whose strongest impression of that country was that the White South Africans *barked* at each other. They were, he thought, so much in the habit of shouting orders or admonitions to their servants that it affected their manner of speech to each other as well. 'Nobody there is gentle any more.' he said. What brought his remark back to my mind was its reverse. In a broadcast on the anniversary of the Soviet invasion of Czechoslovakia a speaker looked back to the summer of 1968 in Prague as one in which, as she put it, 'Everyone had become more gentle, more considerate. Crime and violence diminished. We all seemed to be making a special effort to make life tolerable, just because it had been so intolerable before.'

Now that the Prague Spring and the Czechoslovak long hot summer have retreated into history, we tend to forget – though the Czechs will not forget – the change in the *quality* of ordinary life, while the historians, busy with the politicians floating on the surface of events, or this or that memorandum from a Central Committee or a Praesidium, tell us nothing about what it felt like for people in the streets. At the time John Berger wrote of the immense impression made on him by the transformation of values: 'Workers in many places spontaneously offered to work for nothing on Saturdays in order to contribute to the national fund. Those for whom, a few months before, the highest ideal was a consumer society, offered money and gold to help save the national economy. (Economically a naive gesture but ideologically a significant one.) I saw crowds of workers in the streets of Prague, their faces lit by an evident sense of opportunity and achievement. Such an atmosphere was bound to be temporary. But it was an unforgettable indication of the previously unused potential of a people: of the speed with which demoralisation may be overcome.'[8] And Harry Schwartz of the *New York Times* reminds us that 'Gay, spontaneous, informal and relaxed were the words foreign correspondents used to describe the vast outpouring of merry Prague citizens.'[9] What was Dubcek doing at the time? 'He was trying to set limits on the spontaneous revolution that had been set in motion and to curb it. No doubt he hoped to honour the promises he had given at Dresden that he would impose order on what more and more conservative Communists were calling "anarchy".[10]When the Soviet tanks rolled in to impose *their* order, the spontaneous revolution gave way to a spontaneous resistance. Of Prague, Kamil Winter declared, 'I must confess to you that nothing was organised at all. Everything went on spontaneously ....'[11] And of the second day of the invasion in Bratislava, Ladislav Mňačko wrote: 'Nobody had given any order. Nobody was giving any orders at all. People knew of their own accord what ought to be done. Each and every one of them was his own government, with its orders and regulations, while the government itself was somewhere very far away, probably in Moscow. Everything the occupation forces tried to paralyse went on working and even worked better than in normal times; by the evening the people had even managed to deal with the bread situation'.[12]

In November, when the students staged a sit-in in the universities, 'the sympathy of the population with the students was shown by the dozens of trucks sent from the factories to bring them food free of charge,'[13] and 'Prague's railway workers threatened to strike if the government took reprisal measures against the students. Workers of various state organisations supplied them with food. The buses of the urban transport workers were placed at the strikers' disposal ... Postal workers established certain free telephone communications between university towns.'[14]

The same brief honeymoon with anarchy was observed twelve years earlier in Poland and Hungary. The economist Peter Wiles (who was in Poznan at the time of the bread riots and who went to Hungary in the period when the Austrian frontier was open) noted what he called an 'astonishing moral purity' and he explained:

> Poland had less chance to show this than Hungary, where for weeks there was no authority. In a frenzy of anarchist self-discipline the people, including the criminals, stole nothing, beat no Jews, and never got drunk. They went so far as to lynch only security policemen (AVH) leaving other Communists untouched ... The moral achievement is perhaps unparalleled in revolutionary history ... It was indeed intellectuals of some sort that began both movements, with the industrial workers following them. The peasants had of course never ceased to resist since 1945, but from the nature of things, in a dispersed and passive manner. Peasants stop things, they don't start them. Their sole initiative was the astonishing and deeply moving despatch of free food to Budapest after the first Soviet attack had been beaten.[15]

A Hungarian eyewitness of the same events declared:

> May I tell you one thing about this common sense of the street, during these first days of the revolution? Just, for example, many hours standing in queues for bread and even under such circumstances not a single fight. One day we were standing in a queue and then a truck came with two young boys with machine guns and they were asking us to give them any money we could spare to buy bread for the fighters. All the queue was collecting half a truck-full of bread. It is just an example. Afterwards somebody beside me asked us to hold his place for him because he gave all his money and he had to go home to get some. In this case the whole queue gave him all the money he wanted. Another example: naturally all the shop windows broke in the first days, but not a single thing inside was touched by anybody. You could have seen broken-in shop windows and candy stores, and even the little children didn't touch anything in it. Not even camera shops, opticians or jewellers. Not a single thing was touched for two or three days. And in the streets on the third and fourth day, shop windows were empty, but it was written there that, 'The caretaker has taken it away', or 'Everything from here is in this or that flat.' And in these first days it was a custom to put big boxes on street corners or on crossings where more streets met, and just a script over them 'This is for the wounded, for the casualties or for the families of the dead,' and they were set out in the morning.and by noon they were full of money ...[16]

In Havana, when the general strike brought down the Batista regime and before Castro's army entered the city, a despatch from Robert Lyon, Executive Secretary of the New England office of the American Friends Service Committee, reported that 'There are no police anywhere in the country, but the crime rate is lower than it has been in years,'[17] and the

BBC's correspondent reported that 'The city for days had been without police of any sort, an experience delightful to everyone. Motorists – and considering that they were Cubans this was miraculous – behaved in an orderly manner. Industrial workers, with points to make, demonstrated in small groups, dispersed and went home; bars closed when the customers had had enough and no one seemed more than normally merry. Havana, heaving up after years under a vicious and corrupt police control, smiled in the hot sunshine.'[18]

In all these instances, the new regime has built up its machinery of repression, announcing the necessity of maintaining order and avoiding counter-revolution: 'The Praesidium of the Central Committee of the CPC, the Government and the National Front unequivocally rejected the appeals of the statement of *Two Thousand Words,* which induce to anarchist acts, to violating the constitutional character of our political reform.'[19] And so on, in a variety of languages. No doubt people will cherish the interregnum of elation and spontaneity merely as a memory of a time when, as George Orwell said of revolutionary Barcelona, there was 'a feeling of having suddenly emerged into an era of equality and freedom when human beings were trying to behave like human beings and not as cogs in the capitalist machine,'[20] or when, as Andy Anderson wrote of Hungary in 1956, 'In the society they were glimpsing through the dust and smoke of the battle in the streets, there would be no Prime Minister, no government of professional politicians, and no officials or bosses ordering them about.'[21]

Now you might think that in the study of human behaviour and social relations these moments when society is held together by the cement of human solidarity alone, without the dead weight of power and authority, would have been studied and analysed with the aim of discovering what kind of preconditions exist for an increase in social spontaneity, 'participation' and freedom. The moments when there aren't even any police would surely be of immense interest, if only for criminologists. Yet you don't find them discussed in the texts of social psychology and you don't find them written about by the historians. You have to dig around for them among the personal impressions of people who just happened to be there.

If you want to know why the historians neglect or traduce these moments of revolutionary spontaneity, you should read Noam Chomsky's essay 'Objectivity and Liberal Scholarship'[22] The example he uses is one of the greatest importance for anarchists, the Spanish revolution of 1936, whose history, he remarks, is yet to be written. In looking at the work in this field of the professional historians, he writes: 'It seems to me that there is more than enough evidence to show that a deep bias against social revolution and a commitment to the values and social order of liberal bourgeois democracy has led the author to misrepresent

37

crucial events and to overlook major historical currents.' But this is not his main point. 'At least this much is plain,' he says, 'there are dangerous tendencies in the ideology of the welfare state intelligentsia who claim to possess the technique and understanding required to manage our "post-industrial society" and to organise an international society dominated by American superpower. Many of these dangers are revealed, at a purely ideological level, in the study of the counter-revolutionary subordination of scholarship. The dangers exist both insofar as the claim to knowledge is real and insofar as it is fraudulent. Insofar as the technique of management and control exists, it can be used to diminish spontaneous and free experimentation with new social forms, as it can limit the possibilities for reconstruction of society in the interests of those who are now, to a greater or lesser extent dispossessed. Where the techniques fail, they will be supplemented by all of the methods of coercion that modern technology provides, to preserve order and stability.'

As a final example of what he calls spontaneous and free experimentation with new social forms, let me quote from the account he cites of the revolution in the Spanish village of Membrilla:

> 'In its miserable huts live the poor inhabitants of a poor province; eight thousand people, but the streets are not paved, the town has no newspaper, no cinema, neither a cafe nor a library. On the other hand, it has many churches that have been burned.' Immediately after the Franco insurrection, the land was expropriated and village life collectivised. 'Food, clothing, and tools were distributed equitably to the whole population. Money was abolished, work collectivised, all goods passed to the community, consumption was socialised. It was, however, not a socialisation of wealth but of poverty.' Work continued as before. An elected council appointed committees to organise the life of the commune and its relations to the outside world. The necessities of life were distributed freely, insofar as they were available. A large number of refugees were accommodated. A small library was established, and a small school of design. The document closes with these words: 'The whole population lived as in a large family; functionaries, delegates, the secretary of the syndicates, the members of the municipal council, all elected, acted as heads of a family. But they were controlled, because special privilege or corruption would not be tolerated. Membrilla, is perhaps the poorest village of Spain, but it is the most just'.[23]

And Chomsky comments: 'An account such as this, with its concern for human relations and the ideal of a just society, must appear very strange to the consciousness of the sophisticated intellectual, and it is therefore treated with scorn, or taken to be naive or primitive or otherwise irrational. Only when such prejudice is abandoned will it be possible for historians to undertake a serious study of the popular movement that transformed Republican Spain in one of the most remarkable social revolutions that history records.' There is an order imposed by terror, there is an order enforced by bureaucracy (with the policeman in the corridor) and there is an order which evolves spontaneously from the fact that we are gregarious animals capable of shaping our own destiny. When the first two are absent, the third, as infinitely more human and humane form of order has an opportunity to emerge. Liberty, as Proudhon said, is the mother, not the daughter of order.

Chapter III

THE DISSOLUTION OF LEADERSHIP

Accustomed as is this age to artificial leadership … it is difficult for it to realise the truth that leaders require no training or appointing, but emerge spontaneously when conditions require them. Studying their members in the free-for-all of the Peckham Centre, the observing scientists saw over and over again how one member instinctively became, and was instinctively but not officially recognised as, leader to meet the needs of one particular moment. Such leaders appeared and disappeared as the flux of the Centre required. Because they were not consciously appointed, neither (when they had fulfilled their purpose) where they consciously overthrown. Nor was any particular gratitude shown by members to a leader either at the time of his services or after for services rendered. They followed his guidance just as long as his guidance was helpful and what they wanted. They melted away from him without regrets when some widening of experience beckoned them on to some fresh adventure, which would in turn throw up its spontaneous leader, or when their self-confidence was such that any form of constrained leadership would have been a restraint to them.

JOHN COMERFORD, *Health the Unknown:*
The Story of the Peckham Experiment

Take me to your leader! This is the first demand made by Martians to Earthlings, policemen to demonstrators, journalists to revolutionaries. 'Some journalists', said one of them to Daniel Cohn-Bendit, 'have described you as the leader of the revolution...' He replied, 'Let them write their rubbish. These people will never be able to understand that the student movement doesn't need any chiefs. I am neither a leader nor a professional revolutionary. I am simply a mouthpiece, a megaphone.' Anarchists believe in leaderless groups, and if this phrase is familiar it is because of the paradox that what was known as the leaderless group technique was adopted in the British and Australian armies during the war – and in industrial management since then – as a means of selecting

40

leaders. The military psychologists learned that what they considered to be leader or follower traits are not exhibited in isolation. They are, as one of them wrote, 'relative to a specific social situation – leadership varied from situation to situation and from group to group.' Or as the anarchist, Michael Bakunin, put it over a hundred years ago: 'I receive and I give – such is human life. Each directs and is directed in his turn. Therefore there is no fixed and constant authority, but a continual exchange of mutual, temporary and, above all, voluntary authority and subordination.'

Don't be deceived by the sweet reasonableness of all this. The anarchist concept of leadership is completely revolutionary in its implications – as you can see if you look around, for you will see everywhere in operation the opposite concept: that of hierarchical, authoritarian, privileged and permanent leadership. There are very few comparative studies available of the effects of these two opposite approaches to the organisation of work. Two of them are mentioned in Chapter XI. Another comes from the architectural profession. The Royal Institute of British Architects sponsored a report on the methods of organisation in architects' offices.[1] The survey team felt able to distinguish two opposite approaches to the process of design, which gave rise to very different ways of working and methods of organisation. 'One was characterised by a procedure which began by the invention of a building shape and was followed by a moulding of the client's needs to fit inside this three-dimensional preconception. The other began with an attempt to understand fully the needs of the people who were to use the building around which, when they were clarified, the building would be fitted.'

For the first type, once the basic act of invention and imagination is over, the rest is easy and the architect makes decisions quickly, produces work to time and quickly enough to make a reasonable profit. 'The evidence suggests that this attitude is the predominant one in the group of offices which we found to be using a centralised type of work organisation, and it clearly goes with rather autocratic forms of control.' But 'the other philosophy – from user's needs to building form – makes decision making more difficult ... . The work takes longer and is often unprofitable to the architect, although the client may end up with a much cheaper building put up more quickly than he had expected. Many offices working in this way had found themselves better suited by a *dispersed* type of work organisation which can promote an informal atmosphere of free-flowing ideas . . .' The team found that (apart from a small 'hybrid' group of large public offices with a very rigid and hierarchical structure, a poor quality of design, poor technical and managerial efficiency) the offices surveyed could be classed as either centralised or dispersed types. Staff turnover, which bore no relation at all to earnings, was high in the centralised offices and low or very low in the dispersed ones, where there was considerable delegation of responsibiliy to assistants, and where we found a lively working atmosphere'.

This is a very live issue among architects and it was not a young revolutionary architect but Sir William Pile, when he was head of the Architects and Buildings Branch of the Ministry of Education, who specified among the things he looked for in a member of the building team that 'He must have a belief in what I call the non-hierarchical organisation of the work. The work has got to be organised not on the star system but on the repertory system. The team leader may often be junior to a team member. That will only be accepted if it is commonly accepted that primacy lies with the best idea and not with the senior man.' Again from the architectural world, Walter Gropius proclaimed what he called the technique of 'collaboration among men, which would release the creative instincts of the individual instead of smothering them. The essense of such technique should be to emphasise individual freedom of initiative, instead of authoritarian direction by a boss ... synchronising individual effort by a continuous give and take of its members ...'[2]

Similar findings to those of the RIBA survey come from comparative studies of the organisation of scientific research. Some remarks of Wilhelm Reich on his concept of 'work democracy' are relevant here. I am bound to say that I doubt if he really practised the philosophy he describes, but it certainly corresponds to my experience of working in anarchist groups. He asks, '. . . On what principle, then, was our organisation based, if there were no votes, no directives and commands, no secretaries, presidents, vicepresidents, etc.?' And he answers:

> What kept us together was our *work*, our mutual interdependencies in this work, our factual interest in one gigantic problem with its many specialist ramifications. I had not solicited co-workers. They had come of themselves. They remained, or they left when the work no longer held them. We had not formed a political group or worked out a programme of action . . . Each one made his contribution according to his interest in the work . . . There are, then, objective biological work interests and work functions capable of regulating human co-operation. Exemplary work organises its forms of functioning organically and spontaneously, even though only gradually, gropingly and often making mistakes. In contra-distinction, the political organisations, with their 'campaigns' and 'platforms' proceed without any connection with the tasks and problems of daily life.[3]

Elsewhere in his paper on 'work democracy' he notes that: 'If personal enmities, intrigues and political manoeuvres make their appearance in an organisation, one can be sure that its members no longer have a factual meeting ground in common, that they are no longer held together by a common work interest ... Just as organisational ties result from common work interests, so they dissolve when the work interests dissolve or begin to conflict with each other.'[4]

This fluid, changing leadership derives from authority, but this authority derives from each person's self-chosen function in performing the task in hand. You can be *in* authority, or you can be *an* authority, or you can *have* authority. The first derives from your rank in some chain of command, the second derives from special knowledge, and the third from special wisdom. But knowledge and wisdom are not distributed in order of rank, and they are no one person's monopoly in any undertaking. The fantastic inefficiency of any hierarchial organisation – any factory, office, university, warehouse or hospital – is the outcome of two almost invariable characteristics. One is that the knowledge and wisdom of the people at the bottom of the pyramid finds no place in the decision-making leadership hierarchy of the institution. Frequently it is devoted to making the institution work in spite of the formal leadership structure, or alternatively to sabotaging the ostensible function of the institution, because it is none of their choosing. The other is that they would rather not be there anyway: they are there through economic necessity rather than through identification with a common task which throws up its own shifting and functional leadership.

Perhaps the greatest crime of the industrial system is the way in which it systematically thwarts the inventive genius of the majority of its workers. As Kropotkin asked, 'What can a man invent who is condemned for life to bind together the ends of two threads with the greatest celerity, and knows nothing beyond making a knot?'

> At the outset of modern industry, three generations of workers *have* invented; now they cease to do so. As to the inventions of the engineers, specially trained for devising machines, they are either devoid of genius or not practical enough . . . None but he who knows the machine – not in its drawings and models only, but in its breathing and throbbings – who unconsciously thinks of it while standing by it, can really improve it. Smeaton and Newcomen surely were excellent engineers; but in their engines a boy had to open the steam valve at each stroke of the piston; and it was one of those boys who once managed to connect the valve with the remainder of the machine, so as to make it open automatically, while he ran away to play with the other boys. But in the modern machinery there is no room left for naive improvements of that kind. Scientific education on a wide scale has become necessary for further inventions, and that education is refused to the workers. So that there is no issue out of the difficuly, unless scientific education and handicraft are combined together – unless integration of knowledge takes the place of the present divisions.[5]

The situation today is actually worse than Kropotkin envisaged. The divorce between design and execution, between 'manager' and worker, is more complete. Most people in fact are 'educated' beyond their level in the industrial pyramid. Their capacity for invention and innovation is not wanted by the system. 'You're not paid to think, just get on with it,' says the foreman. 'We are happy that we have re-established the most fundamental principle – management's right to manage,' said Sir Alick Dick when he took over as chairman of the Standard Motor Company (only to be 'resigned' himself when Leylands decided to manage instead).

The remark I value most among the things that were said about the anarchist journal I used to edit, was that of a reviewer who remarked that it was concerned with 'the way in which individual human beings are prevented from developing' and that 'at the same time there is a vision of the unfulfilled potentialities of every human being'.[6] However much this described the intention rather than the result, the sentiment is true. People do go from womb to tomb without ever realising their human potential, precisely because the power to initiate, to participate in innovating, choosing, judging, and deciding is reserved for the top men. It is no accident that the examples I have given of leadership revolving around functional activities come from 'creative' occupations like architecture or scientific research. If ideas are your business, you cannot afford to condemn most of the people in the organisation to being merely machines programmed by somebody else.

But why are there these privileged enclaves where different rules apply?

Creativity is for the gifted few: the rest of us are compelled to live in the environments constructed by the gifted few, listen to the gifted few's music, use the gifted few's inventions and art, and read the poems, fantasies and plays by the gifted few. This is what our education and culture condition us to believe, and this is a culturally induced and perpetuated lie.[7]

The system makes its morons, then despises them for their ineptitude, and rewards its 'gifted few' for their rarity.

Chapter IV

HARMONY THROUGH COMPLEXITY

People like simple ideas and are right to like them. Unfortunately, the simplicity they seek is only to be found in elementary things; and the world, society, and man are made up of insoluble problems, contrary principles, and conflicting forces. Organism means complication, and multiplicity means contradiction, opposition, independence.

P.-J. PROUDHON, *The Theory of Taxation* (1861)

One of the most frequently met reasons for dismissing anarchism as a social theory is the argument that while one can imagine it existing in a small, isolated, primitive community it cannot possibly be conceived in the context of large, complex, industrial societies. This view misunderstands both the nature of anarchism and the nature of tribal societies. Certainly the knowledge that human societies exist, or have existed, without government, without institutionalised authority, and with social and sexual codes quite different from those of our own society, is bound to interest the advocates of anarchy if only to rebut the suggestion that their ideas run contrary to 'human nature', and you will often find quoted in the anarchist press some attractive description of a tribal anarchy, some pocket of the Golden Age (seen from the outside) among the Eskimo, innocent of property, or the sex-happy Trobrianders.

An impressive anthology could be made of such items, as the travel books and works of popular anthropology roll off the presses – from *Aku-Aku* to *Wai-Wai*. Several anarchist writers of the past did just this: Kropotkin in his chapter on 'Mutual Aid Among Savages', Elie Reclus in his *Primitive Folk* and Edward Carpenter in his essay on 'Non-governmental Society', but anthropology has developed its techniques and methods of analysis greatly since the days of the anecdotal approach with its accumulation of travellers' tales. Today, when we view the 'simpler' societies we realise that they are not simple at all. When early Western travellers first came back from African journeys they wrote of the cacophonous sound of the savage jungle drums, or of the primitive mud and straw huts, in patronising or pitying tones because they were blinkered by assumptions about their own society's superiority which blinded them to the subtlety and wonder of other people's culture. Nowadays you can spend a lifetime exploring the structure of African music or the ingenuity and variety of African architecture. In the same way early observers described as sexual promiscuity or group marriage what was simply a different kind of family organisation, or labelled certain societies as anarchistic when a more searching examination might show that they had as effective methods of social control and its enforcement as any authoritarian society, or that certain patterns of behaviour are so rigidly enforced by custom as to make alternatives unthinkable.

The anarchist, in making use of anthropological data today, has to ask more sophisticated questions than his predecessors about the role of law in such societies. But what constitutes 'the law'? Raymond Firth writes: 'When we turn to the sphere of primitive law, we are confronted by difficulties of definition. There is usually no specific code of legislation, issued by a central authority, and no formal judicial body of the nature of a court. Nevertheless there are rules which are expected to be obeyed and which, in fact, are normally kept, and there are means for ensuring some degree of obedience.'[1]

On the classification of these rules and the definition of law anthropologists are divided. By the test of the jurist, who equates the law with what is decided by the courts, 'primitive people have no *law*, but simply a body of customs'; to the sociologists what is important is the whole body of rules of all sorts that exist in a society and the problem of their functioning. Malinowski included in primitive law 'all types of binding obligation and any customary action to prevent breaches in the pattern of social conformity'. Godfrey Wilson takes as the criterion of legal action 'the entry into an issue of one or more members of a social group who are not themselves personally concerned', though others would call the kind of adjudication of a dispute by a senior kinsman or respected neighbour, which Wilson described among the Nyakysua, not law but private arbitration. Indeed Kropotkin in his essay *Law and Authority* singles this out as the antithesis of law: 'Many travellers have depicted the manners of absolutely independent tribes, where laws and chiefs are unknown, but where the members of the tribe have given up stabbing one another in every dispute, because the habit of living in society has ended by developing certain feelings of fraternity and oneness of interest, and they prefer appealing to a third person to settle their differences.'[2]

Wilson, however, sees 'law' as the concomitant of this habit of living in society, defining it as 'that customary force which is kept in being by the inherent necessities of systematic co-operation among its members'. Finally, the school of thought represented by Radcliffe-Brown restricts the sphere of law to 'social control through the systematic application of the force of politically organised society'. But what kind of political organisation? Evans-Pritchard and Meyer Fortes distinguished three types of political system in traditional African societies. Firstly, those like that of the Bushmen where the largest political units embrace people who are all related by kinship so that 'political relations are co-terminous with kinship relations', secondly, those with 'specialised political authority that is institutionalised and vested in roles attached to a state administration', and thirdly, those where political authority is uncentralised. In them 'the political system is based upon a balance of power between many small groups which, with their lack of classes or specialised political offices, have been called *ordered anarchies*'. Several African societies which are law-less in this sense – in that there are no patterns for formal legislation nor for juridical decisions, and which have no law-enforcement officers of any kind – are described in the symposium *Tribes Without Rulers*.[3]

The Tiv, a society of 800,000 people who live on either side of the Benue River in Northern Nigeria were studied by Laura Bohannan. The political attitudes of the Tiv are conveyed in two expressions, to 'repair the country' and to 'spoil the country'. Dr Bohannan explains that 'any act which disturbs the smooth course of social life – war, theft, witchcraft, quarrels – spoils the country; peace, restitution, successful arbitration repairs it'. And she warns that if we try 'to isolate certain attributes of the roles of elders or men of influence as political, we falsify their true social and cultural position . . . I mean this in a positive and not a negative way: a segmentary system of this sort functions not despite but through the absence of an indigenous concept of "the political". Only the intricate interrelations of interests and loyalties through the interconnection of cultural ideology, systems of social grouping, and organisation of institutions and the consequent moral enforcement of each by the other, enables the society to work.'[4]

The Dinka are a people numbering some 900,000 living on the fringe of the central Nile basin in the Southern Sudan. (A correspondent of *The Sunday Times* remarked of them that 'touchiness, pride and reckless disobedience are their characteristic reaction towards authority'.) Godfrey Lienhardt's contribution to *Tribes Without Rulers* describes their intricately subdivided society and the very complicated inter-relationships resulting from the fusion and fission of segments in different combinations for different economic and functional purposes.

It is a part of Dinka political theory that when a subtribe for some reason prospers and grows large, it tends to draw apart politically from the tribe

of which it was a part and behave like a distinct tribe. The sections of a
large subtribe similarly are thought to grow politically more distant from
each other as they grow larger, so that a large and prosperous section of a
subtribe may break away from other sections . . . In the Dinka view, the
tendency is always for their political segments, as for their agnatic
genealogical segments, to grow apart from each other in the course of
time and through the increase in population which they suppose time to
bring.[5]

The Dinka explain their cellular sub-division with such phrases as 'It
became too big, so it separated' and 'They were together long ago but
now they have separated.' They value the unity of their tribes and
descent groups but at the same time they value the feeling for autonomy
in the component segments which lead to fragmentation, and Dr
Lienhardt observes that 'these values of personal autonomy and of its
several sub-segments are from time to time in conflict'.

From a totally different African setting comes Ernest Gellner's
description of the system of trial by collective oath which operated until
recently among the Berber tribes of the Atlas mountains:

This system originally functioned against a background of anarchy; there
was no law-enforcing agency. But whilst there was nothing resembling a
state, there was a society, for everyone recognised, more or less, the
same code, and recognised, more or less, the universal desirability of
pacific settlements of disputes ... Suppose a man is accused of an offence
by another: the man can clear himself of the charge by bringing a set of
men, co-jurors so to speak, to testify in a fixed order, according to
family proximity in the male line to the man on trial ... The rule, the
decision procedure, so to speak, is that if some of the co-jurors fail to
turn up, or fail to testify, or make a slip while testifying, the whole oath
is invalid and the case is lost. The losing party is then obliged to pay the
appropriate fine, determined by custom. In some regions, the rule is
even stranger: those co-jurors who failed to turn up, or failed when
testifying are liable for the fine, rather than the testifying group as a
whole.[6]

How strange, Mr Gellner remarks, that this system should work at all.
Not only by contrast with the legal procedures we are familiar with, but
in view of the possible motives of the participants. One would expect
the co-jurors always to testify for their clansman, whether they thought
him to be innocent or guilty. Yet the system did work, not merely
because the tribesmen believed perjury a sin, punishable by supernatural
forces, but because other social forces are at work. 'We must remember
that each of the two groups is just as anarchic internally as the two are in
their external relations with each other: neither internally nor externally

is there a law-and-order-enforcement machinery, though there is a recognised law and a recognised obligation to respect law and order. In fact this distinction between internal and external politics does not apply.' And the system was applied in disputes at any level, between two families or between tribal confederacies numbered in tens of thousands.

> Given this anarchy, this lack of enforcement within as well as without the group, one way short of violence or expulsion which a clan or family have of disciplining one of their own number is by letting him down at the collective oath. Far from never having a motive for letting down a clansman, or only a transcendental one, they may in fact frequently have such a motive: a habitual offender within their own number may be a positive danger to the group. If he repeats his offences he may well provoke surrounding groups into forming a coalition against it – if, that is, his own group habitually stands by him at the collective oath.

They may do it the first time but the second time they may, even at their own expense, decide to teach him a lesson though it imposes a legal defeat on themselves. Thus trial by collective oath can be a 'genuine and sensitive decision procedure whose verdict is a function of a number of things, amongst which justice is one but not the only one'. Mr Gellner develops his account of this extraordinarily subtle system at great length. The threat of the collective oath is often enough to settle the issue out of court, and the oath itself 'does indeed give any determined, cohesive clan the veto on any decision that would, in virtue of that cohesion, be unenforceable anyway; on the other hand, however, it gives groups the possibility of half-throwing culprits to the wolves, of giving in gracefully, or disciplining the unruly member without actually having to expel him or kill him.' The strange system of social control he describes provides, not a series of totally unenforceable judgments, but at least a half-loaf of justice. One common misconception, he concludes, is that 'the situation in anarchic contexts would be improved if only the participants could overcome their clan or bloc loyalty, if only, instead of 'my clan or bloc, right or wrong', they would think and act as individuals … It seems to me, on the contrary, that unless and until there is genuine enforcement, only blocs or clans can make an anarchic system work.'

Now my purpose in describing the handling of social conflict in non-governmental societies is not to suggest that we should adopt collective oaths as a means of enforcing social norms, but to emphasise that it is not anarchy but government which is a crude simplification of social organisation, and that the very complexity of these tribal societies is the condition of their successful functioning. The editors of *Tribes Without Rulers* summarise the implications in these terms:

In societies lacking ranked and specialised holders of political authority the relations of local groups to one another are seen as a balance of power, maintained by competition between them. Corporate groups may be arranged hierarchically in a series of levels; each group is significant in different circumstances and in connection with different social activities – economic, ritual and governmental. Relations at one level are competitive in one situation, but in another the formerly competitive groups merge in mutual alliance against an outside group. A group at any level has competitive relations with others to ensure the maintenance of its own identity and the rights that belong to it as a corporation, and it may have internal administrative relations that ensure coherence of its constituent elements. The aggregates that emerge as units in one context are merged into larger aggregates in others ...[7]

The 'balance of power' is in fact the method by which social equilibrium is maintained in such societies. Not the balance of power as conceived in nineteenth-century international diplomacy, but in terms of the resolution of forces, exemplified by the physical sciences. Harmony results not from unity but from complexity. It appears, as Kropotkin put it:

as a temporary adjustment established among all forces acting upon a given spot – a provisory adaption. And that adjustment will only last under one condition: that of being continually modified; of representing every moment the resultant of all conflicting actions ...

Under the name of anarchism, a new interpretation of the past and present life of society arises ... It comprises in its midst an infinite variety of capacities, temperaments and individual energies: it excludes none. It even calls for struggles and contentions; because we know that periods of contests, so long as they were freely fought out without the weight of constituted authority being thrown on one side of the balance, were periods when human genius took its mightiest flights ...

It seeks the most complete development of individuality combined with the highest development of voluntary association in all its aspects, in all possible degrees, for all imaginable aims; ever changing, ever modified associations which carry in themselves the elements of their durability and constantly assume new forms which answer best to the multiple aspirations of all. A society to which pre-established forms, crystallised by law, are repugnant; which looks for harmony in an ever-changing and fugitive equilibrium between a multitude of varied forces and influences of every kind, following their own course ...[8]

Anarchy is a function, not of a society's simplicity and lack of social organisation, but of its complexity and multiplicity of social organisations. Cybernetics, the science of control and communication systems, throws valuable light on the anarchist conception of complex self-organising systems. If we must identify biological and political systems, wrote the neurologist Grey Walter, our own brains would seem to illustrate the capacity and limitations of an anarchosyndicalist community: 'We find no boss in the brain, no oligarchic ganglion or glandular Big Brother. Within our heads our very lives depend on equality of opportunity, on specialisation with versatility, on free communication and just restraint, a freedom without interference. Here too, local minorities can and do control their own means of production and expression in free and equal intercourse with their neighbours.'[9] His observations led John D. McEwan to pursue the cybernetic model further. Pointing to the relevance of the Principle of Requisite Variety ('if stability is to be attained the variety of the controlling system must be at least as great as the variety of the system to be controlled') he cites Stafford Beer's illustration of the way in which conventional managerial ideas of organisation fail to satisfy this principle. Beer imagines a visitor from Mars who examines the activities at the lower levels of some large undertaking, the brains of the workers concerned, and the organisational chart which purports to show how the undertaking is controlled. He deduces that the creatures at the top of the hierarchy must have heads yards wide. McEwan contrasts two models of decision-making and control:

First we have the model current among management theorists in industry, with its counterpart in conventional thinking about government in society as a whole. This is the model of a rigid pyramidical hierarchy, with lines of 'communication and command' running from the top to the bottom of the pyramid. There is fixed delineation of responsibility, each element has a specified role, and the procedures to be followed at any level are determined within fairly narrow limits, and may only be changed by decisions of elements higher in the hierarchy. The role of the top group of the hierarchy is sometimes supposed to be comparable to the 'brain' of the system.

The other model is from the cybernetics of evolving self-organising systems. Here we have a system of large variety, sufficient to cope with a complex, unpredictable environment. Its characteristics are changing structure, modifying itself under continual feedback from the environment, exhibiting 'redundancy of potential command', and involving complex interlocking control structures. Learning and decision-making are distributed throughout the system, denser perhaps in some areas than in others.[10]

The same cybernetic criticism of the hierarchical, centralised, governmental concept of organisation has come more recently (and in rather more opaque language) from Donald Schon in his 1970 Reith Lectures. He writes that 'the centre-periphery model has been the dominant model in our society for the growth and diffusion of organisations defined at high levels of specificity. For such a system, the uniform, simple message is essential. The system's ability to handle complex situations depends upon a simple message and upon growth through uniform replication.' Like the anarchists, he sees as an alternative, *networks* 'of elements connecting through one another rather than to each other through a centre', characterised 'by their scope, complexity, stability, homogeneity and flexibility' in which 'nuclei of leadership emerge and shift' with 'the infrastructure powerful enough for the system to hold itself together... without any central facilitator or supporter ...'[11]

Alone among the reviewers of Donald Schon's lectures Mary Douglas perceived the connection with non-governmental tribal societies:

> Once anthropologists thought that if a tribe has no central authority it had no political unity. We were thoroughly dominated by centre theory and missed what was under our noses. Then in 1940 Professor Evans-Pritchard described the Nuer political system and Professor Fortes the Tallensi. They analysed something uncannily close to Schon's Movement or network system: a political structure with no centre and no head, loosely held together by the opposition of its parts. Authority was diffused through the entire population. In each case politics were conducted in an idiom of high generality, the idiom of kinship, which sat very loosely to the political facts. In different contexts, different versions of their governing principles had only a family resemblance. The system was invincible and flexible.[12]

Thus both anthropology and cybernetic theory support Kropotkin's contention that in a society without government, harmony would result from 'an ever-changing adjustment and readjustment of equilibrium between the multitudes of forces and influences' expressed in 'an interwoven network, composed of an infinite variety of groups and federations of all sizes and degrees, local, regional, national and international – temporary or more or less permanent – for all possible purposes: production, consumption and exchange, communications, sanitary arrangements, education, mutual protection, defence of the territory, and so on; and on the other side, for the satisfaction of an ever-increasing number of scientific, artistic, literary and sociable needs.'[13]

How crude the governmental model seems by comparison, whether in social administration, industry, education or economic planning. No wonder it is so unresponsive to actual needs. No wonder, as it attempts to solve its problems by fusion, amalgamation, rationalisation and co-ordination, they only become worse because of the clogging of the lines of communication. The anarchist alternative is that of fragmentation, fission rather than fusion, diversity rather than unity, a mass of societies rather than a mass society.

Chapter V

TOPLESS FEDERATIONS

The fascinating secret of a well-functioning social organism seems thus to lie not in its overall unity but in its structure, maintained in health by the life-preserving mechanism of division operating through myriads of cell-splittings and rejuvenations taking place under the smooth skin of an apparently unchanging body. Wherever, because of age or bad design, this rejuvenating process of subdivision gives way to the calcifying process of cell unification, the cells, now growing behind the protection of their hardened frames beyond their divinely allotted limits, begin, as in cancer, to develop those hostile, arrogant great-power complexes which cannot be brought to an end until the infested organism is either devoured, or a forceful operation succeeds in restoring the small-cell pattern.

LEOPOLD KOHR, *The Breakdown of Nations*

People used to smile at Kropotkin when he instanced the lifeboat institution as an example of the kind of organisation envisaged by anarchists, but he did so simply to illustrate that voluntary and completely non-coercive organisations could provide a complex network of services without the principle of authority intervening. Two other examples which we often use to help people to conceive the federal principle which anarchists see as the way in which local groups and associations could combine for complex functions without any central authority are the postal service and the railways. You can post a letter from here to China or Chile, confident that it will arrive, as a result of freely arrived-at agreements between different national post offices, without there being any central world postal authority at all. Or you can travel across Europe over the lines of a dozen railway systems – capitalist and communist – co-ordinated by agreement between different railway undertakings, without *any kind* of central railway authority. The same is true of broadcasting organisations and several other kinds of internationally co-ordinated activities. Nor is there any reason to suppose that the constituent parts of complex federations could not run efficiently on the basis of voluntary association. (When we have in Britain more than one railway line running scheduled services on time, co-ordinating with British Rail, and operated by a bunch of amateurs, who dare say that the railwaymen could not operate their services without the aid of the bureaucratic hierarchy?) Even within the structure of capitalist industry there are interesting experiments in organising work on the basis of small autonomous groups. Industrial militants regard such ventures with suspicion, as well they might, for they are undertaken not with the idea of stimulating workers' autonomy but with that of increasing productivity. But they are valuable in illustrating our contention that the whole pyramid of hierarchial authority, which has been built up in industry as in every other sphere of life, is a giant confidence trick by which generations of workers have been coerced in the first instance, hoodwinked in the second, and finally brainwashed into accepting.

In territorial terms, the great anarchist advocate of federalism was Proudhon who was thinking not of customs unions like the European Common Market nor of a confederation of states or a world federal government but of a basic principle of human organisation:

> In his view the federal principle should operate from the simplest level of society. The organisation of administration should begin locally and as near the direct control of the people as possible; individuals should start the process by federating into communes and associations. Above that primary level the confederal organisation would become less an organ of administration than of coordination between local units. Thus the nation would be replaced by a geographical confederation of regions, and Europe would become a confederation of confederations, in which the interest of the smallest province would have as much expression as that of the largest, and in which all affairs would be settled by mutual agreement, contract, and arbitration. In terms of the evolution of anarchist ideas, *Du Principe Federatif* (1863) is one of the most important of Proudhon's books, since it presents the first intensive libertarian development of the idea of federal organisation as a practical alternative to political nationalism.[1]

Now without wishing to sing a song of praise for the Swiss political system we can see that, in territorial terms, the twenty-two sovereign cantons of Switzerland are an outstanding example of a successful federation. It is a federation of like units, of small cells, and the cantonal boundaries cut across the linguistic and ethnic boundaries, so that unlike the many examples of unsuccessful political federation, the confederation is not dominated by a single powerful unit, so different in size and scale from the rest that it unbalances the union. The problem of federalism, as Leopold Kohr puts it in his book *The Breakdown of Nations*, is one of division, not of union. Proudhon foresaw this:

> Europe would be too large to form a single confederation; it would have to be a confederation of confederations. This is why I pointed out in my most recent publication (*Federation and Unity in Italy*) that the first measure of reform to be made in public law is the re-establishment of the Italian, Greek, Batavian (Netherlands), Scandinavian and Danubian confederations as a prelude to the decentralisation of the large States, followed by a general disarmament. In these conditions all nations would recover their freedom, and the notion of the balance of power in Europe would become a reality. This has been envisaged by all political writers and statesmen but has remained impossible so long as the great powers are centralised States. It is not surprising that the notion of federation should have been lost amid the splendours of the great States, since it is by nature peaceful and mild and plays a self-effacing role on the political scene.[2]

Peaceful, mild and self-effacing the Swiss may be and we may consider them a rather stodgy and provincial lot, but they have something in their national life which we in the nations which are neither mild nor self-effacing have lost. I was talking to a Swiss citizen (or rather a citizen of Zurich, for strictly speaking that is what he was) about the cutting-back to profitable inter-city routes of the British railway system, and he remarked that it would be inconceivable in a Swiss setting that a chairman in London could decide, as Dr Beeching did in the 1960s, to write off the railway system of the north of Scotland. He cited Herbert Luethy's study of his country's political system in which he explained that:

> Every Sunday the inhabitants of scores of communes go to the polling booths to elect their civil servants, ratify such and such an item of expenditure, or decide whether a road or a school should be built; after settling the business of the commune, they deal with cantonal elections and voting on cantonal issues; lastly … come the decisions on federal issues. In some cantons the sovereign people still meet in Rousseau-like fashion to discuss questions of common interest. It may be thought that this ancient form of assembly is no more than a pious tradition with a certain value as a tourist attraction. If so, it is worth looking at the results of local democracy.
>
> The simplest example is the Swiss railway system, which is the densest network in the world. At great cost and with great trouble it has been made to serve the needs of the smallest localities and most remote valleys, not as a paying proposition but because such was the will of the people. It is the outcome of fierce political struggles. In the nineteenth

century the 'democratic railway movement' brought the small Swiss communities into conflict with the big towns, which had plans for centralisation ...

And if we compare the Swiss system with the French which, with admirable geometrical regularity, is entirely centred on Paris so that the prosperity or the decline, the life or death, of whole regions has depended on the quality of the link with the capital we see the difference between a centralised state and a federal alliance. The railway map is the easiest to read at a glance, but let us now superimpose on it another showing economic activity and the movement of population. The distribution of industrial activity all over Switzerland, even in the outlying areas, accounts for the strength and stability of the social structure of the country and prevented those horrible nineteenth-century concentrations of industry, with their slums and rootless proletariat.[3]

I suspect that times have changed, even in Switzerland, and quote Dr Luethy, not to praise Swiss democracy, but to indicate that the federal principle which is at the centre of anarchist theory is worth very much more attention than it is given in the textbooks on political science. Even in the context of ordinary political and economic institutions, its adoption has a far-reaching effect. If you doubt this, consult an up-to-date map of British Rail.

The federal principle applies to every kind of human organisation You can readily see its application to communications of all kinds: a network of local papers sharing stories, a network of local radio and television stations supported by local listeners (as already happen with a handful of stations in the United States) sharing programmes,[4] a network of local telephone services (it already happens in Hull which through some historical anomaly runs its own telephone system and gives its citizens a rather better service than the Post Office gives the rest of us).

It already applies in the world of voluntary associations, unions, and pressure groups, and you will not disagree that the lively and active ones are those where activity and decision-making is initiated at local level, while those that are centrally controlled are ossified and out of touch with their apathetic membership. Those readers who remember the days of CND and the Committee of 100 may recall the episode of the Spies for Peace. A group of people unearthed details of the RSGs or Regional Seats of Government, underground hide-outs to ensure the survival of the ruling elite in the case of nuclear war. It was of course illegal to publish this information, yet all over the country it appeared in little anonymous duplicated pamphlets within a few days, providing an enormously interesting example of *ad hoc* federal activity through loose networks of active individuals. We later published in *Anarchy* some reflections on the implications of this:

One lesson to be drawn from 'Spies for Peace' is the advantage of *ad hoc* organisation, coming rapidly into being and if necessary disappearing with the same speed, but leaving behind innumerable centres of activity, like ripples and eddies on a pond, after a stone has been thrown into it.

Traditional politics (both 'revolutionary' and 'reformist') are based on a central dynamo, with a transmission belt leading outwards. Capture of the dynamo, or its conversion to other purposes, may break the transmission entirely. 'Spies for Peace' seems to have operated on an entirely different basis. Messages were passed from mouth to mouth along the route, documents from hand to hand. One group passed a secret to a second, which then set about reprinting it. A caravan became the source of a leaflet, a shopping basket a distribution centre. A hundred copies of a pamphlet are distributed in the streets: some are sure to reach the people who will distribute them.

Contacts are built on a face to face basis. One knows the personal limitations of one's comrades. X is an expert at steering a meeting through procedural shoals, but cannot work a duplicator. Y can use a small printing press, but is unable to write a leaflet. Z can express himself in public, but cannot sell pamphlets. Every task elects its own workers, and there is no need for an elaborate show of hands. Seekers of personal power and glory get little thrill from the anonymously and skilfully illegal. The prospect of prison breeds out the leader complex. Every member of a group may be called upon to undertake key tasks. And all-round talent is developed in all. The development of small groups for mutual aid could form a basis for an effective resistance movement.

There are important conclusions. Revolution does not need conveyor belt organisation. It needs hundreds, thousands, and finally millions of people meeting in groups with informal contacts with each other. It needs mass consciousness. If one group takes an initiative that is valuable, others will take it up. The methods must be tailored to the society we live in. The FLN could use armed warfare, for it had hills and thickets to retreat into. We are faced by the overwhelming physical force of a State better organised and better armed than at any time in its history. We must react accordingly. The many internal contradictions of the State must be skilfully exploited. The Dusseldorf authorities were caught in their own regulations when the disarmers refused to fasten their safety belts. MI5 cannot conceive of subversion that is not master-minded by a sinister Communist agent. It is incapable of dealing with a movement where nobody takes orders from anyone else. Through action, autonomy and revolutionary initiative will be developed still further. To cope with our activities the apparatus of repression will become even more centralised and even more bureaucratic. This will enhance our opportunities rather than lessen them.[5]

This was a federation whose members did not even know each other, but whose constituent cells had an intimate personal understanding. The passport to membership was simply a common involvement in a common task. Innumerable voluntary organisations from the Scouts to the Automobile Association started in the same impromptu way. Their ossification began from the centre. Their mistake was a faith in centralism. The anarchist conclusion is that every kind of human activity should begin from what is local and immediate, should link in a network with no centre and no directing agency, hiving off new cells as the original ones grow. If there is any human activity that does not appear to fit this pattern our first question should be 'Why not?' and our second should be 'How can we re-arrange it so as to provide for local autonomy, local responsibility, and the fulfilment of local needs?'

Chapter VI

WHO IS TO PLAN?

Urban development is the capitalist definition of space. It is one particular real-isation of the technically possible, and it excludes all alternatives. Urban studies should be seen — like aesthetics, whose path to complete confusion they are about to follow — as a rather neglected type of penal reform: an epidemiology of the social disease called revolt.

The 'theory' of urban development seeks to enlist the support of its victims, to persuade them that they have really chosen the bureaucratic form of conditioning expressed by modern architecture. To this end, all the emphasis is placed on utility, the better to hide the fact that this architecture's real utility is to control men and reify the relations between them. People need a roof over their heads: superblocks provide it. People need informing and entertaining: telly does just that. But of course the kind of information, entertainment and place to live which such arguments help sell are not created for people at all, but rather without them and against them.

KOTANYI and VANEIGEM, *Theses on Unitary Urbanism*

Contemporary town planning had its origins in the sanitary reform and public health movements of the nineteenth century, overlaid by architectural notions about civic design, economic notions about the location of industry, and above all by engineering notions about highway planning. Today, when there are close links between official planners and speculative developers, to the corruption of the former and the enrichment of the latter, we forget that there was also, in the early ideologists of town planning like Patrick Geddes and Ebenezer Howard, the hope of a great popular movement for town improvement and city development, and for a regionalist and decentralist approach to physical planning. There was even a link with anarchism through the persons of anarchist geographers like Kropotkin and Elisee Reclus and their friendship with Patrick Geddes (whose biographer writes: 'an

59

interesting book could be written about the scientific origins of the international anarchist movement, and if it were, the name of Geddes would not be absent'.)[1]

But, in a society where urban land and its development are in the hands of speculative entrepreneurs and where the powers of urban initiative are in the hands of local and national government, it was inevitable that the processes of change and innovation should be controlled by bureaucracies and speculators or by an alliance between the two. With not the slightest provision for popular initiative and choice in the whole planning process it is scarcely surprising that the citizen mistrusts and fears the 'planner' who for him is just one more municipal functionary working in secrecy in City Hall.

When the poor working-class districts of our cities were devastated by bombing in the Second World War it was said that Hitler had provided the opportunity for massive slum clearance and reconstruction which could never have been achieved in peace-time. Comprehensive redevelopment of the bombed areas was undertaken. But so wedded was the planning profession and its municipal employers to the huge, utilitarian rehousing project that they proceeded with their own *blitzkrieg*, with the demolition contractor taking the place of the bomber.

'Raze and rise' was their crude philosophy, a terrible simplification of the historical process of urban decay and renewal, as though the intention was to obliterate the fact that our cities had a past. And it was pursued with the thoroughness of total war, as you can see with surrealist clarity in a city like Liverpool where hundreds of acres have been devastated while neither the Corporation nor anyone else has the finance for rebuilding. They either sow grass on the flattened streets or deposit rubble to keep out the Gypsies. Another aspect of the war of planning against the poor has been the universal policy of building inner ring roads or urban motorways for the benefit of the out-of-town commuter and the motoring lobby. The highway engineer has staked his professional reputation on getting the traffic through – at whatever cost – and, needless to say, it is the poor districts of the city that provide the cheapest route.

In the United States similar policies of urban renewal have meant the destruction of the run-down, down-town sector of town to replace low-income housing by office blocks, parking lots or expensive apartments at high rents. In practice, 'bringing back life to the city' meant 'running the Blacks out of town'. What happened to the inhabitants unable to afford the new high rents? Obviously they were squeezed into the remaining run-down districts, thus increasing their housing problems. The result, apart from the long, hot summers of the late 1960s, was a revulsion against the idea of 'planning', and the growth of the idea of the planner, not as the servant of the powerful interests that govern the city but as the advocate of the inhabitants, to help them formulate their own plan, or at least their own demands on City Hall.

The same loss of faith in 'planning' led to the provisions in current British legislation for 'public participation in planning'.[2] So foreign are these mildly democratic notions to the way things are actually managed in a formally democratic society that many of the early attempts at promoting 'advocacy planning' have been seen as yet another subtle form of manipulation, of gaining a community's acquiescence in its own destruction, while in Britain the planning profession's interpretation of public participation has simply meant *informing* the public of what is in store once the basic decisions have already been taken. In urban rehousing the planners congratulate themselves on abandoning the inhuman and grossly uneconomic tower block housing policy only to institute urban rehabilitation policies which in practice have meant that landlords, aided by government grants, have rehabilitated their property, 'winkled out' the original tenants and either let the improved properties at middle-class rents or sold them to middle-class purchasers. Their former tenants are added to the numbers of overcrowded or homeless city dwellers, compelled by their low incomes to be the superfluous people, the non-citizens of the city who man its essential services at incomes that do not allow them to live there above the squalor level.

Planning, the essential grid of an ordered society which, it is said, makes anarchy 'an impossible dream', turns out to be yet another way in which the rich and powerful oppress and harass the weak and poor. The disillusionment with planning as a plausible activity has led to quite serious suggestions that we would be better off without it, not merely, as would be predictable, from the free market entrepreneurs, resenting any limitation on their sacred right to make maximum profits, but from involved professionals. One such group in Britain flew a kite labelled 'Non-Plan: An Experiment in Freedom'. Why not have the courage, they asked, to let people shape their own environment? And they declared that:

> The whole concept of planning (the town and country kind at least) has gone cock-eyed. What we have today represents a whole cumulation of good intentions. And what those good intentions are worth, we have almost no way of knowing . . . As Melvin Webber has pointed out: planning is the only branch of knowledge purporting to be a science which regards a plan as being *fulfilled* when it is merely *completed;* there's seldom any sort of check on whether the plan actually does what it was meant to do, and whether, if it does something different, this is for the better or for the worse.[3]

They illustrate this with examples of the way in which many of the aspects of the physical environment that we admire today were developed for absolutely different reasons, which the planner never foresaw. Most planning, they declare, is aristocratic or oligarchical in its methods. At a deeper level Richard Sennett has written a book, *The Uses of Disorder*, which led one critic to declare that 'with this book the process of redefining nineteenth-century anarchism for the twentieth century is begun'. Several different threads of thought are woven together in Sennett's study of 'personal identity and city life'. The first is a notion that he derives from the psychologist Erik Erikson that in adolescence men seek a purified identity to escape from uncertainty and pain and that true adulthood is found in the acceptance of diversity and disorder. The second is that modern American society freezes men in the adolescent posture – a gross simplification of urban life in which, when rich enough, people escape from the complexity of the city, with its problems of cultural diversity and income disparity, to private family circles of security in the suburbs – the purified community. The third is that city planning as it has been conceived in the past – with techniques like zoning and the elimination of 'non-conforming users' – has abetted this process, especially by projecting trends into the future as a basis for present energy and expenditure.

This means guessing the future physical and social requirements of a community or city and then basing present spending and energy so as to achieve a readiness for the projected future state. In planning schools, beginning students usually argue that people's lives in time are wandering and unpredictable, that societies have a history in the sense that they do what was not expected of them, so that this device is misleading. Planning teachers usually reply that of course the projected need would be altered by practical objections in the course of being worked out; the projective-need analysis is a pattern of ideal conditions rather than a fixed prescription.

But the facts of planning in the last few years have shown that this disclaimer on the part of planners is something that they do not really mean. Professional planners of highways, of redevelopment housing, of inner-city renewal projects have treated challenges from displaced communities or community groups as a threat to the value of their plans rather than as a natural part of the effort at social reconstruction. Over and over again one can hear in planning circles a fear expressed when the human beings affected by planning changes become even slightly interested in the remedies proposed for their lives. 'Interference', 'blocking', and 'interruption of work' – these are the terms by which social challenges or divergencies from the planners' projections are interpreted. What has really happened is that the planners have wanted to take the plan, the projection in advance, as more 'true' than the historical turns, the unforeseen movements in the real time of human lives.[4]

His prescription for overcoming the crisis of American cities is a reversal of these trends, a move for 'outgrowing a purified identity'. He wants cities where people are forced to confront each other: 'There would be no policing, nor any other form of central control, of schooling, zoning, renewal, or city activities that could be performed through common community action, or even more importantly, through direct, non-violent conflict in the city itself.' Non-violent? Yes, because Sennett claims that the present, modern, affluent city is one in which aggression and conflict are denied outlets other than violence, precisely because of the lack of personal confrontation. (Cries for law and order are loudest when communities – in the American suburb – are most isolated from other people in the city.) The clearest example, he suggests, of the way this violence occurs 'is found in the pressures on the police in modern cities. Police are expected to be bureaucrats of hostility resolution' but 'a society that visualises the lawful response to disorder as an impersonal, passive coercion only invites terrifying outbreaks of police rioting'. Whereas the anarchist city that he envisages, 'pushing men to say what they think about each other in order to forge some mutual pattern of compatibility', is not a compromise between order and violence but a wholly different way of living in which people wouldn't have to choose between the two:

> Really 'decentralised' power, so that the individual has to deal with those around him, in a milieu of diversity, involves a change in the essence of communal control, that is, in the refusal to regulate conflict. For example, police control of much civil disorder ought to be sharply curbed; the responsibility for making peace in neighbourhood affairs ought to fall on the people involved. Because men are now so innocent and unskilled in the expression of conflict, they can only view these disorders as spiralling into violence. Until they learn through experience that the handling of conflict is something that cannot be passed on to policemen, this polarisation and escalation of conflict into violence will be the only end they can frame for themselves. This is as true of those who expect police reprisals against themselves, like the small group of militant students, as those who call in the police 'on their side'[5]

The professional's task is changed too. 'Instead of planning for some abstract urban whole, planners are going to have to work for the concrete parts of the city, the different classes, ethnic groups and races it contains. And the work they do for these people cannot be laying out their future; the people will have no chance to mature unless they do that for themselves, unless they are actively involved in shaping their social lives.'

The emphasis shifts from the distant city planning authority to the local community association and the growth and growing sophistication of such associations is a hopeful pointer in the direction of Sennett's urban anarchy. We already have examples, both in Britain and in the United States, of community groups (with no 'official' status) developing their own rehousing plans, just as feasible as those of the local authority, but more in tune with the desires of tenants, and capable, even under present-day conditions, of financial viability through housing society finance. The next step is the Neighbourhood Council idea, and the step after that is for neighbourhoods to achieve real control of neighbourhood facilities. After that comes the federation of neighbourhoods.

The paradox here is that you can see the usual indifference and low electoral turn-out for the local authority elections and, at the same time, widespread support for and interest in an *ad hoc* community action group which devotes much of its time to fighting the local authority. From an anarchist point of view this is not surprising. The council, polarised on political party lines, remote from the neighbourhood, dominated by its professional officials who, as Chris Holmes said, operate the machinery in such a way as to make local initiative fruitless, is the descendent of nineteenth-century squirearchical paternalism. The Community Association, springing up from real concern over real issues, operates on the scale of face-to-face groups, and for this very reason is invested with a kind of popular legitimacy.

Ioan Bowen Rees, in the course of his valuable book *Government by Community*, compares the timid recommendations of the Skeffington Report on public participation in planning with current practice in Switzerland: 'It was with the public that the Swiss began, with the Parish Meeting, as it were, passing its own planning statute and approving its own development plan.' The person who is intoxicated by large-scale thinking asks how planning could operate under these conditions. Well, Mr Bowen Rees emphasises, 'No community in Switzerland is insignificant. This means that a small commune can – and sometimes does – hold up a motorway. And also that a small commune can – and sometimes does – save itself from economic stagnation by its own efforts. And why not? The result is neither poverty nor chaos.'[6]

The idea of social planning and social administration through a decentralised network of autonomous communities is not a new idea, it is a return to a very old one. Walter Ullmann remarks that the towns of the Middle Ages 'represent a rather clear demonstration of entities governing themselves' and that: 'In order to transact business, the community assembled in its entirety ... the assembly was not "representative" of the whole, but was the whole.' He describes the antipathy between federations of autonomous communes and the central authorities:

That the communes, the *communitates,* became the target of attack by the 'establishment' is not difficult to understand. In some instances the word 'commune' was even employed as a term of abuse . . . From the point of view of autonomy it is understandable why and how the towns entered into alliances, also called *conjurationes,* or leagues with other towns. The populist complexion of the towns perhaps tended to harbour a certain revolutionary spirit, directed against the wielders of the *Obrigkeit,* against Authority.[7]

The early history of the United States was a period when in local administration the Town Meeting was supreme. As Tom Paine wrote: 'For upwards of two years from the commencement of the American War, and for a longer period in several of the American states, there were no established forms of government. The old governments had been abolished and the country was too much occupied in defence to employ its attention in establishing new governments; yet during this interval order and harmony were preserved as inviolate as in any country of Europe.'[8] And Staughton Lynd comments: 'In the American tradition, too, rebellion against inherited authorities was not mere "anti-institutionalism". Implicit, sometimes explicit, in the American revolutionary tradition was a dream of the good society as a voluntary federation of local communal institutions, perpetually recreated from below by what Paul Goodman calls "a continuous series of existential constitutional acts".'[9]

The rediscovery of community power, arising from the enormities of centralised bureaucratic planning, could be the beginning of a re-creation of this tradition. And it is precisely because we are in the very early stages of rediscovering it in a society dominated by bureaucratic administration that we have to learn through experience the pitfalls and disappointments of community organisation without community power, community consultation as a diversion from real community action. In Barnsbury, in North London, middle-class amenity pressure groups succeeded in getting traffic shifted into adjoining working-class districts where community pressure was less vocally organised. Here, of course, there is an answer, given years ago in another context by the traffic pundit, Professor Buchanan: 'Sandbag a few streets, and see what happens.'[10]

An American planner, Sherry Arnstein, devised a 'ladder of participation' as a means of evaluating the genuineness or spuriousness of schemes for community participation in planning.[11] The rungs of her ladder are:

CITIZEN CONTROL
DELEGATED POWER
PARTNERSHIP
PLACATION
CONSULTATION
INFORMING
THERAPY
MANIPULATION

Arnstein's ladder is a very useful device for cutting our ideas about participation down to size. The Skeffington Report, especially as translated into practice, is only up to rungs three or four of the ladder. Its emphasis is on *educating* the public to an understanding of the planning authorities. It says, 'we see the process of giving information and opportunities for participation as one which leads to a greater understanding and co-operation rather than to a crescendo of dispute'. But a crescendo of dispute is precisely what we need if we are ever to climb the rungs of Arnstein's ladder to full citizen control.

Chapter VII

WE HOUSE, YOU ARE HOUSED, THEY ARE HOMELESS

In English, the word 'housing' can be used as a noun or as a verb. When used as a noun, housing describes a commodity *or* product. *The verb 'to house' describes the* process *or* activity *of housing . . .*

Housing problems are defined by material standards, and housing values are judged by the material quantity of related products, such as profit or equity. From the viewpoint of a central planner or an official designer or administrator, these are self-evident truths . . .

According to those for whom housing is an activity, these conclusions are absurd. They fail to distinguish between what things are, *materially speaking, and what they* do *in people's lives. This blindness, which pervades all institutions of modern society explains the stupidity of tearing down 'sub-standard' houses or 'slums' when their occupants have no other place to go but the remaining slums, unless, of course, they are forced to create new slums from previously 'standard' homes. This blindness also explains the monstrous 'low-cost' projects (which almost always turn out to have very high costs for the public as well as for the unfortunate 'beneficiaries').*

JOHN TURNER, 'Housing as a Verb' in *Freedom to Build*

Ours is a society in which, in every field, one group of people makes decisions, exercises control, limits choices, while the great majority have to accept these decisions, submit to this control and act within the limits of these externally imposed choices. Nowhere is this more evident than in the field of housing: one of those basic human needs which throughout history and all over the world people have satisfied as well as they could for themselves, using the materials that were at hand and their own, and their neighbours' labour. The marvellously resourceful anonymous vernacular architecture of every part of the globe is a testimony to their skill, using timber, straw, grass, leaves, hides, stone, clay, bone, earth, mud and even snow. Consider the igloo: maximum enclosure of space with minimum of labour. Cost of materials and transportation, nil. And all made of water. Nowadays, of course, the eskimos live on welfare handouts in little northern slums. Man, as Habraken says, 'no longer houses himself: he is housed.'[1]

Even today 'a third of the world's people house themselves with their own hands, sometimes in the absence of government and professional intervention, sometimes in spite of it.'[2] In the rich nations the more advances that are made in building technology and the more complex the financial provision that is made for housing, the more intractable the 'problem' becomes. In neither Britain nor the United States has huge public investment in housing programmes met the needs of the poorest citizens. In the Third World countries of Asia, Africa and Latin America the enormous movement of population into the big cities during the last two decades has resulted in the growth of huge peripheral squatter settlements around the existing cities, inhabited by the 'invisible' people who have no official urban existence. Pat Crooke points out that cities grow and develop on two levels, the official, theoretical level and the popular, actual, unofficial level, and that the majority of the population of many Latin American cities are unofficial citizens with a 'popular economy' outside the institutional financial structure of the city. Here is Barbara Ward's description of these unofficial cities, *colonias proletarias* as they are called in Mexico, *barriadas* in Peru, *gourbivilles* in Tunis, *bustees* in India, *gecekondu* in Turkey, *ranchos* in Venezuela:

> Drive from the neo-functional glass and concrete of any big-city airport in the developing world to the neo-functional glass and concrete of the latest big-city hotel and somewhere in between you are bound to pass one or other of the sectors in which half and more of the city-dwellers are condemned to live.
>
> Sometimes the modern highway passes above them. Looking down, the traveller catches a glimpse, under a pall of smoke from cooking pots in back-yards, of mile on mile of little alleys snaking through densely packed huts of straw, crumbling brick or beaten tin cans. Or the main road slices through some pre-existent shanty-town and, for a brief span, the visitor looks down the endless length of rows of huts, sees the holes, the mud, the rubbish in the alleyways, skinny chickens picking in the dirt, multitudes of nearly naked children, hair matted, eyes dull, spindly legs, and, above them, pathetic lines of rags and torn garments strung up to dry between the stunted trees.[3]

Well, that is how it looks to the visitor. The local official citizens don't even notice the invisible city. But does it feel like that on the ground to the inhabitant, making a place of his own, as a physical foothold in urban life and the urban economy? The official view, from city officials, governments, newspapermen, and international agencies, is that such settlements are the breeding-grounds for every kind of crime, vice, disease, social and family disorganisation. How could they not be since they sprang up without official sanction or finance and as the result of illegal seizure of land? The reality is different:

> Ten years of work in Peruvian *barriadas* indicates that such a view is grossly inaccurate: although it serves some vested political and bureau-cratic interests, it bears little relation to reality . . . Instead of chaos and disorganisation, the evidence instead points to highly organised inva-sions of public land in the face of violent police opposition, internal political organisation with yearly local elections, thousands of people living together in an orderly fashion with no police protection or public services. The original straw houses constructed during the invasions are converted as rapidly as possible into brick and cement structures with an investment totalling millions of dollars in labour and materials. Employment rates, wages, literacy, and educational levels are all higher than in central city slums (from which most *barriada* residents have escaped) and higher than the national average. Crime, juvenile delin-quency, prostitution and gambling are rare, except for petty thievery, the incidence of which is seemingly smaller than in other parts of the city.[4]

Such reports could be quoted from the squatter experience of many parts of the world. These authors, John Turner and William Mangin, ask the obvious question: can the *barriada* – a self-help, mass migration community development by the poor, be exported to, for example, the United States: 'Some observers, under the impression that the govern-ments of Peru, Brazil, Chile, Turkey, Greece and Nigeria had adopted the *barriada* movements as a policy for solving these same problems, have thought the US could do the same. In fact, these governments' main role in *barriada* formation has been their lack of ability to *prevent* mass invasions of land. They are simply not powerful enough nor sure enough of their own survival to prevent invasions by force. In the United States, the government is firmly entrenched and could prevent such action. Moreover, every piece of land is owned by someone, usually with a clear title . . .'[5] They point too to the lessons of Oscar Lewis's *The Culture of Poverty:* that putting people into government housing projects does little to halt the economic cycle in which they are entrapped, while 'when people move on their own, seize land, and build their own houses and communities, it has considerable effect'. Lewis's evidence shows that many social strengths, as well as 'precarious but real economic security' were lost when people were moved from the self-created communities of San Juan into public housing projects. 'The rents and the initial investment for public housing are high, at the precise time the family can least afford to pay. Moreover, public housing is created by architects, planners, and economists who would not be caught dead living in it, so that the inhabitants feel no psychological or spiritual claim on it.'[6]

In the US, Turner and Mangin conclude, the agencies that are supposedly helping the poor, in the light of Peruvian experience, actually seem to be *keeping* them poor.

The poor of the Third World shanty-towns, acting anarchically, because no authority is powerful enough to prevent them from doing so, have three freedoms which the poor of the rich world have lost. As John Turner puts it, they have the freedom of community self-selection, the freedom to budget one's own resources and the freedom to shape one's own environment. In the rich world, every bit of land belongs to someone, who has the law and the agents of law-enforcement firmly on his side. Building regulations and planning legislation are rigidly enforced, unless you happen to be a developer who can hire architects and negotiators shrewd enough to find a way round them or who can do a deal with the authorities.

In looking for parallels in British experience, what exactly are we seeking? If it is for examples of defiance of the sacred rights of property, there are examples all through our history. If you go back far enough, all our ancestors must have been squatters and there have continually been movements to assert people's rights to their share of the land. In the seventeenth century a homeless person could apply to the Quarter Sessions who, with the consent of the township concerned, could grant him permission to build a house with a small garden on the common land. The Digger Movement during the Commonwealth asserted this right at George's Hill near Weybridge, and Cromwell's troops burnt down their houses. Our history must be full of unrecorded examples of squatters who were prudent enough to let it be assumed that they had title to the land. It is certainly full of examples of the theft of the common land by the rich and powerful. If we are looking for examples of people building for themselves, self-build housing societies are a contemporary one. If it is simply the application of popular direct action in the field of housing, apart from the squatter movement of 1946, mass rent strikes, like those in Glasgow in 1915 or in East London in 1938, are the most notable examples, and there are certainly going to be more in the future.

At the time of the 1946 squatting campaign, I categorised the stages or phases common to all examples of popular direct action in housing in a non-revolutionary situation. Firstly, *initiative,* the individual action or decision that begins the campaign, the spark that starts the blaze. Secondly, *consolidation,* when the movement spreads sufficiently to consti-tute a threat to property rights and becomes big enough to avoid being snuffed out by the authorities. Thirdly, *success,* when the authorities have to concede to the movement what it has won. Finally, *official action*, usually undertaken unwillingly to placate the popular demand, or to incorporate it in the status quo.[7]

The 1946 campaign was based on the large-scale seizure of army camps emptied at the end of the war. It started in May of that year when some homeless families in Lincolnshire occupied an empty camp, and it spread like wildfire until hundreds of camps were seized in every part of Britain. By October 1,038 camps had been occupied by 40,000 families in England and Wales, and another 5,000 families in Scotland. That month, Aneurin Bevan, the Minister of Health who was responsible for the government's housing programme, accused the squatters of 'jumping their place in the housing queue'. In fact, of course, they were jumping right out of the queue by moving into buildings which would not otherwise have been used for housing purposes. Then suddenly the Ministry of Works, which had previously declared itself not interested, found it possible to offer the Ministry of Health 850 former service camps, and squatting became 'official'.

Some of the original squatter communities lasted for years. Over a hundred families, who in 1946 occupied a camp known as Field Farm in Oxfordshire, stayed together and twelve years later were finally rehoused in the new village of Berinsfield on the same site.

A very revealing account of the differences between the 'official' and the 'unofficial' squatters comes from a newspaper account of a camp in Lancashire after the first winter:

> There are two camps within the camp – the official squatters (that is the people placed in the huts after the first invasion) and the unofficial squatters (the veterans, who have been allowed to remain on sufferance). Both pay the same rent of 10s a week – but there the similarity ends. Although one would have imagined that the acceptance of rent from both should accord them identical privileges, in fact, it does not. Workmen have put up partitions in the huts of the official squatters – and have put in sinks and other numerous conveniences. These are the sheep; the goats have perforce to fend for themselves.
>
> A commentary on the situation was made by one of the young welfare officers attached to the housing department. On her visit of inspection she found that the goats had set to work with a will, improvising partitions, running up curtains, distempering, painting and using initiative. The official squatters, on the other hand, sat about glumly without using initiative or lifting a hand to help themselves and bemoaning their fate, even though they might have been removed from the most appalling slum property. Until the overworked corporation workmen got around to them they would not attempt to improve affairs themselves.[8]

This story reveals a great deal about the state of mind that is induced by free and independent action, and that which is induced by dependence and inertia: the difference between people who initiate things and act for themselves and people to whom things just happen.

The more recent squatters' campaign in Britain had its origins in the participation of the 'libertarian Left' in campaigns in the 1960s over conditions in official reception centres for homeless people, principally the year-long campaign to improve conditions at the King Hill hostel in Kent. 'The King Hill campaign began spontaneously among the hostel inmates, and when outsiders joined it a general principle was that decisions should be taken by the homeless people themselves and the activities should confine their part to giving advice, gathering information, getting publicity and raising support and this pattern has been repeated in every subsequent campaign.'[9] From the success of the King Hill campaign the squatters' movement passed on to the occupation of empty property, mostly belonging to local authorities who had purchased it for eventual demolition for road improvements, car parks, municipal offices, or in the course of deals with developers. This was at first resisted by the authorities, and a protracted lawsuit followed the use of so-called private detectives and security agencies to terrorise and intimidate the squatters. Councils also deliberately destroyed premises, (and are continuing to do so) in order to keep the squatters out. The London Family Squatters Association then applied a kind of Gandhian moral blackmail before the court of public opinion to enforce the collaboration of borough councils in handing over short-term accommodation to squatting families. In some cases, to avoid political embarrassment, councils have simply turned a blind eye to the existence of the squatters.

Just one of the many predictable paradoxes of housing in Britain is the gulf between the owner-occupier and the municipal tenant. Nearly a third of the population live in municipally-owned houses or flats, but there is not a single estate controlled by its tenants, apart from a handful of co-operative housing societies. The owner-occupier cherishes and improves his home, although its space standards and structural quality may be lower than that of the prize-winning piece of municipal architecture whose tenant displays little pride or pleasure in *his* home. The municipal tenant is trapped in a syndrome of dependence and resentment, which is an accurate reflection of his housing situation. People care about what is theirs, what they can modify, alter, adapt to changing needs and improve for themselves. They must be able to attack their environment to make it truly their own. They must have a direct responsibility for it.

As the pressure on municipal tenants grows through the continuous rent increases which they are powerless to oppose except by collective resistance, so the demand will grow for a change in the status of the tenant, and for tenant control. The tenant take-over of the municipal estate is one of those obviously sensible ideas which is dormant because our approach to municipal affairs is still stuck in the grooves of nine-teenth-century paternalism. We have the fully-documented case-history of Oslo in Norway as a guide here. It began with the problems of one of their pre-war estates with low standards, an unpleasant appearance and great resistance to an increase in rents to cover the cost of improvements. As an experiment the estate was turned over to a tenant co-operative, a policy which transformed both the estate and the tenants' attitudes. Now Oslo's whole housing policy is based on this principle. This is not anarchy, but it is one of its ingredients.[10]

Chapter VIII

OPEN AND CLOSED FAMILIES

In choosing a partner we try both to retain the relationships we have enjoyed in childhood, and to recoup ourselves for fantasies which have been denied us. Mate-selection accordingly becomes for many an attempt to cast a particular part in a fantasy production of their own, and since both parties have the same intention but rarely quite the same fantasies, the result may well be a duel of rival producers. There are men, as Stanley Spencer said of himself, who need two complementary wives, and women who need two complementary husbands, or at least two complementary love objects. If we insist first that this is immoral or 'unfaithful', and second that should it occur there is an obligation on each love-object to insist on exclusive rights, we merely add unnecessary difficulties to a problem which might have presented none, or at least presented fewer, if anyone were permitted to solve it in their own way.

ALEX COMFORT, *Sex in Society*

One essentially anarchist revolution that has advanced enormously in our own day is the sexual revolution. It is anarchist precisely because it involves denying the authority of the regulations laid down by the state and by various religious enterprises over the activities of the individual. And we can claim that it has advanced, not because of the 'breakdown' of the family that moralists (quite erroneously) see all around them, but because in Western society more and more people have decided to conduct their sexual lives as they see best. Those who have prophesied dreadful consequences as a result of the greater sexual freedom which the young assert – unwanted babies, venereal disease and so on – are usually the very same people who seek the fulfilment of their prophesies by opposing the free availability to the young of contraception and the removal of the stigma and mystification that surround venereal disease.

The official code on sexual matters was bequeathed to the state by the Christian Church, and has been harder and harder to justify with the decline of the beliefs on which it was based. Anarchists, from Emma Goldman to Alex Comfort, have observed the connection between political and sexual repression and, although those who think sexual liberation is necessarily going to lead to political and economic liberation are probably optimistic, it certainly makes people happier. That there is no immutable basis for sexual codes can be seen from the wide varieties in accepted behaviour and in legislation on sexual matters at different periods and in different countries. Male homosexuality became a 'problem' only because it was the subject of legislation. Female homosexuality was no problem because its existence was ignored by (male) legislators. The legal anomalies are sometimes hilarious: 'Who can explain just why anal intercourse is legal in Scotland between male and female, but illegal between male and male? Why is anal intercourse illegal in England between male and female, yet okay between males if both are over 21?'[1]

The more the law is tinkered with in the effort to make it more rational the more absurdities are revealed. Does this mean that there are no rational codes for sexual behaviour? Of course not: they simply get buried in the irrationalities or devalued through association with irrelevant prohibitions. Alex Comfort, who sees sex as 'the healthiest and most important human sport' suggests that 'the actual content of sexual behaviour probably changes much less between cultures than the individual's capacity to enjoy it without guilt'. He enunciated two moral injunctions or commandments on sexual behaviour: 'Thou shalt not exploit another person's feelings,' and 'Thou shalt under no circumstances cause the birth of an unwanted child.'[2] His reference to 'commandments' led Professor Maurice Carstairs to tease him with the question why, as an anarchist, Comfort was prescribing rules? – to which he replied that a philosophy of freedom demanded higher standards of personal responsibility than a belief in authority. The lack of ordinary prudence and chivalry which could often be observed in adolescent behaviour today was, he suggested, precisely the result of prescribing a code of chastity which did not make sense instead of principles which are 'immediately intelligible and acceptable to any sensible youngster'.

You certainly don't have to be an anarchist to see the modern nuclear family as a straitjacket answer to the functional needs of home-making and child-rearing which imposes intolerable strains on many of the people trapped in it. Edmund Leach remarked that 'far from being the basis of the good society, the family, with its narrow privacy and tawdry secrets, is the source of all our discontents'.[3] David Cooper called it 'the ultimate and most lethal gas chamber in our society', and Jacquetta Hawkes said that 'it is a form making fearful demands on the human beings caught up in it; heavily weighted for loneliness, excessive demands, strain and failure'.[4] Obviously it suits some of us as the best working arrangement but our society makes no provision for the others, whose numbers you can assess by asking yourself the question: 'How many happy families do I know?'

Consider the case of John Citizen. On the strength of a few happy evenings in the discotheque, he and Mary make a contract with the state and/or some religious enterprise to live together for life and are given a licence to copulate. Assuming that they surmount the problems of finding somewhere to live and raise a family, look at them a few years later. He, struggling home from work each day, sees himself caught in a trap. She feels the same, the lonely single-handed housewife, chained to the sink and the nappy-bucket. And the kids too, increasingly as the years go by, feel trapped. Why can't Mum and Dad just leave us alone? There is no need to go on with the saga because you know it all backward.

In terms of the happiness and fulfilment of the individuals involved, the modern family is an improvement on its nineteenth-century predecessor or on the various institutional alternatives dreamed up by authoritarian utopians and we might very well argue that today there is nothing to prevent people from living however they like but, in fact, everything about our society, from the advertisements on television to the laws of inheritance, is based on the assumption of the tight little consumer unit of the nuclear family. Housing is an obvious example: municipal housing makes no provision for non-standard units and in the private sector no loans or mortgages are available for communes.

The rich can avoid the trap by the simple expedient of paying other people to run their households and rear their children. But for the ordinary family the system makes demands which very many people cannot meet. We accept it because it is universal. Indeed the only examples that Dr Leach could cite where children 'grow up in larger, more relaxed domestic groups centred on the community rather than on mother's kitchen' were the Israeli kibbutz or the Chinese commune, so ubiquitous has the pattern become. But changes are coming: the women's liberation movement is one reminder that the price of the nuclear family is the subjugation of women. The communes or joint households that some young people are setting up are no doubt partly a reflection of the need to share inflated rents but are much more a reaction against what they see as the stultifying rigid nature of the small family unit.

The mystique of biological parenthood results in some couples living in desperate unhappiness because of their infertility while others have children who are neglected and unwanted. It also gives rise to the common situation of parents clinging to their children because they have sunk so much of their emotional capital in them while the children desperately want to get away from their possessive love. 'A secure home', writes John Hartwell, 'often means a stifling atmosphere where human relationships are turned into a parody and where signs of creativity are crushed as evidence of deviancy.'[5] We are very far from the kind of community in which children could choose which of the local parent-figures they would like to attach themselves to but a number of interesting suggestions are in the air, all aiming at loosening family ties in the interests of both parents and children. There is the idea of Paul and Jean Ritter of a neighbourhood 'children's house' serving twenty-five to forty families,[6] there is Paul Goodman's notion of a Youth House on the analogy of this institution in some 'primitive' cultures, and there is Teddy Gold's suggested Multiple Family Housing Unit.[7] These ideas are not based on any rejection of our responsibility towards the young; they involve sharing this responsibility throughout the community and accepting the principle that, as Kropotkin put it, *all* children are *our* children. They also imply giving children themselves responsibilities not only for themselves but to the community, which is exactly what our family structure fails to do.

Personal needs and aspirations vary so greatly that it is as fatuous to suggest stereotyped alternatives as it is to recommend universal conformity to the existing pattern. At one end of the scale is the warping of the child by the accident of parenthood, either by possessiveness or by the perpetuation of a family syndrome of inadequacy and incompetence. At the other end is the emotional stultification of the child through a lack of personal attachments in institutional child care. We all know conventional households permeated with casual affection where domestic chores and responsibilities are shared, while we can readily imagine a communal household in which the women were drudges collectively instead of individually and in which a child who was not very attractive or assertive was not so much left alone as neglected. More important than the structure of the family are the expectations that people have of their roles in it. The domestic tyrant of the Victorian family was able to exercise his tyranny only because the others were prepared to put up with it.

There is an old slogan among progressive educators, *Have'em, Love'em and Leave'em Alone.* This again is not urging neglect, but it does emphasise that half the personal miseries and frustrations of adolescents and of the adults they become are due to the insidious pressures on the individual to do what other people think is appropriate for him. At the same time the continual extension of the processes of formal education delays even further the granting of real responsibility to the young. Any teacher in further education will tell you of the difference between sixteen-year-olds who are at work and attend part-time vocational courses and those of the same age who are still in full-time education. In those benighted countries where young children are still allowed to work you notice not only the element of exploitation but also the maturity that goes with undertaking functional responsibilities in the real world.

The young are caught in a tender trap: the age of puberty and the age of marriage (since our society does not readily permit experimental alternatives yet) go down while, at the same time, acceptance into the adult world is continually deferred - despite the lowering of the formal age of majority. No wonder many adults appear to be cast in a mould of immaturity. In family life we have not yet developed a genuinely permissive society but simply one in which it is difficult to grow up. On the other hand, the fact that for a minority of young people – a minority which is increasing – the stereotypes of sexual behaviour and sexual roles which confined and oppressed their elders for centuries have simply become irrelevant, will certainly be seen in the future as one of the positive achievements of our age.

Chapter IX

SCHOOLS NO LONGER

From William Godwin's An Account of the Seminary That Will Be Opened on Monday the Fourth Day of August at Epsom in Surrey *(1783) to Paul Goodman's* Compulsory Mis-education *(1964), anarchism has persistently regarded itself as having distinctive and revolutionary implications for education. Indeed, no other movement whatever has assigned to educational principles, concepts, experiments, and practices a more significant place in its writings and activities.*

KRIMERMAN and PERRY, *Patterns of Anarchy* (1966)

Ultimately the social function of education is to perpetuate society: it is *the* socialising function. Society guarantees its future by rearing its children in its own image. In traditional societies the peasant rears his sons to cultivate the soil, the man of power rears his to wield power, and the priest instructs them all in the necessity of a priesthood. In modern governmental society, as Frank MacKinnon puts it, 'The educational system is the largest instrument in the modern state for telling people what to do. It enrols five-year-olds and tries to direct their mental, and much of their social, physical and moral development for twelve or more of the most formative years of their lives.'[1]

To find a historical parallel to this you would have to go back to ancient Sparta, the principal difference being that the only education we hear of in the ancient world is that of ruling classes. Spartan education was simply training for infantry warfare and for instructing the citizens in the techniques for subduing the slave class, the helots who did the daily work of the state and greatly outnumbered the citizens. In the modern world the helots have to be educated too, and the equivalent of Spartan warfare is the industrial and technical competition between nations which is sometimes the product of war and sometimes its prelude. The year in which Britain's initial advantage in the world's industrial markets began to wane was the year in which, after generations of bickering

about its religious content, universal compulsory elementary education
was introduced, and every significant development since the Act of 1870
had a close relationship to the experience, not merely of commercial
rivalry but of war itself. The English Education Acts of 1902, 1918 and
1944 were all born of war, and every new international conflict, whether
in rivalry for markets or in military techniques, has been the signal for a
new burst of concern among the rival powers over the scale and scope of
their systems of education.

The notion that primary education should be free, compulsory and
universal is very much older than the British legislation of the nineteenth century. Martin Luther appealed 'To the Councilmen of all Cities
in Germany that they establish and maintain Christian schools,' compulsory education was founded in Calvinist Geneva in 1536, and Calvin's
Scottish disciple, John Knox 'planted a school as well as a kirk in every
parish'. In Puritan Massachusetts free compulsory education was introduced in 1647. The common school, Lewis Mumford notes, 'contrary
to popular belief, is no belated product of nineteenth-century democracy: it played a necessary part in the absolutist-mechanical formula ...
centralised authority was now belatedly taking up the work that had
been neglected with the wiping out of municipal freedom in the greater
part of Europe.'[2] In other words, having destroyed local initiative, the
state was acting in its own interest. Compulsory education is bound up
historically, not only with the printing press, the rise of protestantism
and capitalism, but with the growth of the idea of the nation state itself.

All the great rationalist philosophers of the eighteenth century
pondered on the problems of popular education, and the two acutest
educational thinkers among them ranged themselves on opposite sides
on the question of the *organisation* of education: Rousseau for the state,
William Godwin against it. Rousseau, whose *Emile* postulates a
completely individual education (human society is ignored, the tutor's
entire life is devoted to poor Emile) did, nevertheless, in his *Discourse on
Political Economy* (1758) argue for public education 'under regulations
prescribed by the government ... if children are brought up in common
in the bosom of equality; if they are imbued with the laws of the State
and the precepts of the General Will ... we cannot doubt that they will
cherish one another mutually as brothers ... to become in time
defenders and fathers of the country of which they will have been for so
long the children.'

Godwin, in his *Enquiry Concerning Political Justice* (1793) criticises the
whole idea of a *national* education. He summarises the arguments in
favour, which are those used by Rousseau, adding to them the question,
'If the education of our youth be entirely confined to the prudence of
their parents, or the accidental benevolence of private individuals, will it
not be a necessary consequence that some will be educated to virtue,

others to vice, and others again entirely neglected?' Godwin's answer is worth quoting at length because his lone voice from the end of the eighteenth century speaks to us in the accents of the de-schoolers of our own day:

> The injuries that result from a system of national education are, in the first place, that all public establishments include in them the idea of permanence ... public education has always expended its energies in the support of prejudice; it teaches its pupils not the fortitude that shall bring every proposition to the test of examination, but the art of vindicating such tenets as may chance to be previously established ... Even in the petty institution of Sunday schools, the chief lessons that are taught are a superstitious veneration for the Church of England, and to bow to every man in a handsome coat ...
>
> Secondly, the idea of national education is founded in an inattention to the nature of mind. Whatever each man does for himself is done well; whatever his neighbours or his country undertake to do for him is done ill ... He that learns because he desires to learn will listen to the instructions he receives and apprehend their meaning. He that teaches because he desires to teach will discharge his occupation with enthusiasm and energy. But the moment political institution undertakes to assign to every man his place, the functions of all will be discharged with supineness and indifference ...
>
> Thirdly, the project of a national education ought uniformly to be discouraged on account of its obvious alliance with national government ... Government will not fail to employ it to strengthen its hand and perpetuate its institutions ... Their view as instigator of a system of education will not fail to be analogous to their views in their political capacity ...[3]

Contemporary critics of the alliance between national government and national education would agree, and would argue that it is in the *nature* of public authorities to run coercive and hierarchical institutions whose ultimate function is to perpetuate social inequality and to brainwash the young into the acceptance of their particular slot in the organised system. A hundred years ago, in a book called *God and the State*, Michael Bakunin characterised 'the people' as 'the eternal minor, the pupil confessedly forever incompetent to pass his examinations, rise to the knowledge of his teachers, and dispense with their discipline'.

> One day I asked Mazzini what measures would be taken for the emancipation of the people, once his triumphant unitary republic had been definitely established. 'The first measure', he answered, 'will be the foundation of schools for the people.' 'And what will the people be taught in these schools?' 'The duties of man - sacrifice and devotion.'[4]

Bakunin made the same comparison as is made today by Everett Reimer and Ivan Illich between the teaching profession and a priestly caste, and he declared that 'Like conditions, like causes, always produce like effects. It will, then, be the same with the professors of the modern school, divinely inspired and licensed by the State. They will necessarily become, some without knowing it, others with full knowledge of the cause, teachers of the doctrine of popular sacrifice to the power of the State and to the profit of the privileged classes.' Must we then, he asked, eliminate from society all instruction and abolish all schools? Far from it, he replied, but he demanded schools from which the *principle of authority* will be eliminated: 'They will be schools no longer; they will be popular academies in which neither pupils nor masters will be known, where the people will come freely to get, if they need it, free instruction, and in which, rich in their own expertise, they will teach in their turn many things to the professors who shall bring them knowledge which they lack.'[5]

This entirely different conception of the school had already been envisaged by Godwin in 1797 as a plan 'calculated entirely to change the face of education. The whole formidable apparatus, which has hitherto attended it, is swept away. Strictly speaking, no such characters are left upon the scene as either preceptor or pupil. The boy, like the man, studies because he desires it. He proceeds upon a plan of his own invention, or which, by adopting, he has made his own.'[6] Perhaps the nearest thing to a school of this kind within the official system was Prestolee School (an elementary school in Lancashire revolutionised after the First World War by its headmaster Edward O'Neil), where 'time-tables and programmes play an insignificant part, for the older children come back when school hours are over, and with them, their parents and elder brothers and sisters'.[7]

In spite of the talk of 'community schools' there are a thousand bureaucratic reasons why O'Neil's version of Bakunin's 'popular academy' could not be put into practice today, and remains only a vision of the future transformation of the school. However, Professor Harry Rée told a conference of young teachers that: 'I think we are going to see in your lifetime the end of schools as we know them. Instead there will be a community centre with the doors open twelve hours a day, seven days a week, where anybody can wander in and out of the library, workshops, sports centre, self-service store and bar. In a hundred years' time the compulsory attendance laws for children to go to school may have gone the same way as the compulsory laws for attendance at church.'[8]

Today, as the educational budgets of both rich and poor nations get more and more gigantic, we would add a further criticism of the role of the state as educator throughout the world: the affront to the idea of social justice. An immense effort by well-intentioned reformers has gone into the attempt to manipulate the education system to provide equality of opportunity, but this has simply resulted in a theoretical and illusory equal start in a competition to become more and more unequal. The greater the sums of money that are poured into the education industries of the world, the smaller the benefit to the people at the bottom of the educational, occupational and social hierarchy. The universal education system turns out to be yet another way in which the poor subsidise the rich. Everett Reimer, for instance, remarking that schools are an almost perfectly regressive form of taxation, notes that the children of the poorest one-tenth of the population of the United States cost the public in schooling $2,500 each over a lifetime, while the children of the richest one-tenth cost about $35,000. 'Assuming that one-third of this is private expenditure, the richest one-tenth still gets ten times as much of public funds for education as the poorest one-tenth.' In his suppressed Unesco report of 1970 Michael Huberman reached the same conclusion for the majority of countries in the world. In Britain, ignoring completely the university aspect, we spend twice as much on the secondary school life of a grammar-school sixth former as on a secondary modern school-leaver, while, if we do include university expenditure, we spend as much on an undergraduate in one year as on a normal schoolchild throughout his life. 'While the highest social group benefit *seventeen* times as much as the lowest group from the expenditure on universities, they only contribute five times as much revenue.' We may thus conclude that one significant role of the state in the education systems of the world is to perpetuate social and economic injustice.

You can see why one contemporary anarchist educator, Paul Goodman, suggests that it would be simpler, cheaper and fairer to dismantle the system and give each kid his or her share of the education money. Goodman's programme is devastatingly simple. For the young child provide a 'protective and life-nourishing environment, by decentralising the school into small units of twenty to fifty in available shopfronts or clubhouses, with class attendances not compulsory. Link the school with economically marginal farms where city kids can go for a couple of months a year. For older children:

> Probably an even better model would be the Athenian pedagogue touring the city with his charges; but for this the streets and working-places of the city must be made safer and more available than is likely. (The prerequisite of city-planning is for the children to be able to use the city, for no city is governable if it does not grow citizens who feel it is theirs.) The goal of elementary pedagogy is a very modest one: it is for a small child, under his own steam, to poke interestingly into whatever goes on and be able, by observation, questions and practical imitation, to

83

get something out of it in his own terms. In our society this happens pretty well at home up to age four, but after that it becomes forbiddingly difficult.[9]

Technical education, he believes, is best undertaken on the job for, provided that 'the young have options and can organise and criticise, on the job education is the quickest way to workers' management'. University education 'is for *adults* who already know something'.

Goodman peddled his ideas of incidental education in and out of season for most of his writing life, but only very recently have people begun to take them seriously. What has changed the climate has been the experience of the students' revolt, and the educational crisis of the American cities – with more and more expenditure providing less and less effective education, and the impact of educational thinkers from the Third World like Ivan Illich and Paolo Freire who have shown how totally inappropriate to real social needs the standard pattern of school and university are. Everywhere experiments are being made to break away from the straitjacket of Illich's definition of school as the 'age-specific, teacher-related process requiring full-time attendance at an obligatory curriculum'. What inhibits such experiments is precisely the existence of the official system which pre-empts the options of the citizens who are obliged to finance it, so that alternatives are dependent on the marginal income of potential users. When the Scotland Road Free School in Liverpool asked the education authority for some very modest assistance in the form of equipment, one member of the Education Committee declared that 'we are being asked to weaken the fabric of what we ourselves are supposed to be supporting ... We might finish up with the fact that no children will want to go to our schools.'

The anarchist approach to education is grounded, not in a contempt for learning, but in a respect for the learner. Danilo Dolci told me of encountering 'bandits' in Sicily whose one contact with 'education' was learning to read from an anarchist fellow-prisoner in jail. Arturo Barea recalled from his childhood in Madrid two poverty-stricken anarchist pedagogues. One, the Penny Teacher lived in a hut made of petrol cans in the Barrio de las Injurias. A horde of ragged pupils squatted round him in the open to learn the ABC at ten centimos a month. The other, the Saint with the Beard, used to hold his classes in exchange for his pupils' collection of cigarette-ends in the Plaza Mayor. The Penny Teacher was sent to prison as an anarchist and died there. The Saint with the Beard was warned off from his corner and disappeared. But he turned up again eventually and went on secretly lending tattered books to his pupils, for the love of reading.

The most devastating criticism we can make of the organised system is that its effects are profoundly anti-educational. In Britain, at five years old, most children cannot wait to get into school. At fifteen, most cannot wait to get out. On the day I am writing, our biggest-selling newspaper devotes its front page to a photograph of a thirteen-year-old truant, with his comment, 'The worse part is I thought I only had another two years to sweat out, then they put the leaving age up to sixteen. That's when I thought, sod it.' The likeliest lever for change in the organised system will come, not from criticism or example from outside, but from pressure from below. There has always been a proportion of pupils who attend unwillingly, who resent the authority of the school and its arbitrary regulations, and who put a low value on the processes of education because their own experience tells them that it is an obstacle race in which they are so often the losers that they would be mugs to enter the competition. *This* is what school has taught them, and when this army of also-rans, no longer cowed by threats, no longer amenable to cajolery, no longer to be bludgeoned by physical violence into sullen acquiescence grows large enough to prevent the school from functioning with even the semblance of relevance or effectiveness, the educational revolution will begin.

At the opposite end of the educational spectrum, the university, the process of renewal through secession has ancient historical precedents. Oxford was started by seceding English students from Paris, Cambridge by scholars who fled from Oxford, London by dissenters who could not accept the religious qualifications required by Oxford and Cambridge. But the most perfect anarchist model for a university comes from Spain. Towards the end of the last century, the Spanish government, dominated then as now, by the Church, dismissed some leading university professors. A few of them started a 'free' school for higher studies, the *Institución Libre de Enseñanza* and around this arose the so-called 'Generation of '98' the small group of intellectuals who, paralleling the growth of the working class movements of that time, sought to diagnose the stifling inertia, hypocrisy and corruption of Spanish life – the art critic and teacher Manuel Cossío, the philosophers Unamuno and Ortega y Gasset, the economist Joacquín Costa (who summed up his programme for Spain in the phrase *school and larder*) the poet Antonio Machado and the novelist Pío Baroja. The *Institución* had an even more remarkable offspring, the *Residencia de Estudiantes,* or Residential College for Students, founded by Alberto Jiménez in 1910. Gerald Brenan gives us a fascinating glimpse of the *Residencia:*

> Here, over a long course of years, Unamuno, Cossío and Ortega taught, walking about the garden or sitting in the shade of the trees in the manner of the ancient philosophers: here Juan Ramon Jiménez wrote and recited his poems, and here too a later generation of poets, among them Garcia Lorca and Alberti, learned their trade, coming under the

influence of the school of music and folksong which Eduardo Martinez Torner organised. Never, I think, since the early Middle Ages has an educational establishment produced such astonishing results on the life of a nation, for it was largely by means of the *Institución* and the *Residencia* that Spanish culture was raised suddenly to a level it had not known for three hundred years.[10]

Lorca, Dali and Buñuel were fellow students at the *Residencia;* a true community of scholars with a genuine function in the community it served. The only parallels I can think of are the one-time Black Mountain College in the US, and the annual two-day History Workshop at Ruskin College, Oxford (significantly not a part of the university), where at a cost of 50p each a thousand students and teachers gather to present and discuss original research in an atmosphere like that of a pop festival. It is a festival of scholarship, far away from the world of vice-chancellors and academic boards, running a finishing school for the bored aspirants for privileged jobs in the meritocracy.

In the world-wide student revolt of the late 1960s, from one university after another came the comment that the period of revolutionary self-government was the one genuinely educational experience that the students had encountered. 'He had learned more in those six weeks than in four years of classes,' (Dwight Macdonald on a Columbia student); 'Everyone is a richer person for the experience and has enriched the community by it,' (LSE student); 'The last ten days have been the most rewarding of my whole university career,' (Peter Townsend, of Essex University); 'This generation of Hull students has had the opportunity to take part in events which may well be the most valuable part of their university lives,' (David Rubinstein on Hull). At Hornsey College of Art one lecturer said, 'It's the greatest educational thing I've ever known,' and another called it 'a surge of creativity unheard of in the annals of higher education'.

What a delicious, but predictable irony, that *real* education, self-education, should only come from locking out or ignoring the expensive academic hierarchy. The students' revolt was a microcosm of anarchy, spontaneous, self-directed activity replacing the power structure by a network of autonomous groups and individuals. What the students experienced was that sense of liberation that comes from taking your own decisions and assuming your own responsibilities. It is an experience that we need to carry far beyond the privileged world of higher education, into the factory, the neighbourhood, the daily lives of people everywhere.

Chapter X

PLAY AS AN ANARCHIST PARABLE

The boy who swings from rope to horse, leaping back again to the swinging rope, is learning by his eyes, muscles, joints and by every sense organ he has, to judge, to estimate, to know. The other twenty-nine boys and girls in the gymnasium are all as active as he, some of them in his immediate vicinity. But as he swings he does not avoid. He swings where there is space – a very important distinction – and in doing so he threads his way among the twenty-nine fellows. Using all his facilities, he is aware of the total situation in that gymnasium – of his own swinging and of his fellows' actions. He does not shout to the others to stop, to wait or move from him – not that there is silence, for running conversations across the hall are kept up as he speeds through the air. But this 'education' in the live use of all his senses can only come if his twenty-nine fellows are also free and active. If the room were cleared and twenty-nine boys sat at the side silent while he swung, we should in effect be saying to him – to his legs, body, eyes – 'You give all your attention to swinging, we'll keep the rest of the world away'– in fact 'Be as egotistical as you like'. By so reducing the diversity in the environment we should be preventing his learning to apprehend and to move in a complex situation. We should in effect be saying 'Only this and this do; you can't be expected to do more. Is it any wonder that he comes to behave as though it is all he can do? By the existing methods of teaching we are in fact inducing the child's inco-ordination in society.

INNES PEARSE and LUCY CROCKER, *The Peckham Experiment*

All the problems of social life present a choice between libertarian and authoritarian solutions, and the ultimate claim we can make for the libertarian approach is that it fulfils its function better. The adventure playground is an arresting example of this living anarchy; one that is valuable both in itself and as an experimental verification of a whole social approach. The need to provide children's playgrounds as such is a result of high density urban living and fast-moving traffic. The authoritarian response to this need is to provide an area of tarmac and some pieces of expensive ironmongery in the form of swings, see-saws and roundabouts which provide a certain amount of fun (though because of their inflexibility children soon tire of them) but which call for no imaginative or constructive effort on the child's part, and cannot be incorporated in any self chosen or reciprocal activity. Swings and roundabouts can only be used in one way, they cater for no fantasies, for no developing skills, for no emulation of adult activities, they call for no mental effort and very little physical effort, and are giving way to simpler and freer apparatus like climbing frames, log piles, 'jungle gyms', commando nets, or to play-sculptures – abstract shapes to clamber through and over, or large constructions in the form of boats, traction engines, lorries or trains. But these too provide for a limited age range and a restricted range of activities, and are sometimes more indulgent to the designer than to the user. It is not surprising that children find more continual interest in the street, the derelict building or the scrap yard.

For older boys, team games are the officially approved activity – if they can find some permitted place to play them, but as Patrick Geddes wrote before the First World War, 'they are at most granted a cricket pitch or lent a space between football goals but otherwise are jealously watched, as potential savages, who on the least symptom of their natural activities of wigwam-building, cave-digging, stream-damming and so on – must be instantly chivied away, and are lucky if not handed over to the police.'[1]

That there should be anything novel in simply providing facilities for the spontaneous, unorganised activities of childhood is an indication of how deeply rooted in our social behaviour is the urge to control, direct and limit the flow of life. But when they get the chance, in the country, or where there are large gardens, woods, or bits of waste land, what are children doing? Enclosing space, making caves, tents, dens, from old bricks, bits of wood and corrugated iron. Finding some corner which the adult world has passed over, and making it their own. How can children in towns find and appropriate this kind of private world when, as Agnete Vestereg of the Copenhagen Junk Playground writes:

> Every bit of land is put to industrial or commercial use, where every patch of grass is protected or enclosed, where streams and hollows are filled in, cultivated and built on?
>
> But more is done for children now than used to be done, it may be objected. Yes, but that is one of the chief faults – the things are *done*. Town children move about in a world full of the marvels of technical science. They may see and be impressed by things; but they long also to take possession of them, to have them in their hands, to make something themselves, to create and re-create ...[2]

The Emdrup playground was begun in 1943 by the Copenhagen

Workers' Co-operative Housing Association after their landscape architect, C. T. Sorensen, who had laid out many orthodox playgrounds had
observed that children seemed to get more pleasure when they stole into
building sites and played with the materials they found there. In spite of
a daily average attendance of 200 children at Emdrup, and that 'difficult'
children were specially catered for, it was found that 'the noise, screams
and fights found in dull playgrounds are absent, for the opportunities are
so rich that the children do not need to fight'.

The initial success at Copenhagen has led in the years since the war to
a widespread diffusion of the idea and its variations, from 'Freetown' in
Stockholm and 'The Yard' at Minneapolis, to the *Skrammellegeplads* or
building playgrounds of Denmark and the Robinson Crusoe playgrounds of Switzerland, where children are provided with the raw materials and tools for building and for making gardens and sculpture. In
Britain we have had twenty years of experience of the successes and
pitfalls of adventure playgrounds and enough documentation of them to
disabuse anyone who thinks it easy to start and operate an adventure
playground, as well as anyone who thinks it a waste of time.[3]

When The Yard was opened in Minneapolis with the aim of giving
the children 'their own spot of earth and plenty of tools and materials for
digging, building and creating as they see fit',

> it was every child for himself. The initial stockpile of secondhand
> lumber disappeared like ice off a hot stove. Children helped themselves
> to all they could carry, sawed off long boards when short pieces would
> have done. Some hoarded tools and supplies in secret caches. Everybody
> wanted to build the biggest shack in the shortest time. The workman-
> ship was shoddy.
>
> Then came the bust. There wasn't a stick of lumber left. Hijacking
> raids were staged on half-finished shacks. Grumbling and bickering
> broke out. A few children packed up and left.
>
> But on the second day of the great depression most of the youngsters
> banded together spontaneously for a salvage drive. Tools and nails came
> out of hiding. For over a week the youngsters made do with what they
> had. Rugged individualists who had insisted on building alone invited
> others to join in – and bring their supplies along. New ideas popped up
> for joint projects. By the time a fresh supply of lumber arrived a
> community had been born.[4]

The same story could be told of dozens of similar ventures since then.
Sometimes there is what Sheila Beskine called a 'fantastic spontaneous
lease of life' followed by decline and then by renewal in a different direction. But permanence is not the criterion of success. As Lady Allen says,
a good adventure playground 'is in a continual process of destruction and
growth'.

Years ago, when *The Times Educational Supplement* had commented skeptically on such playgrounds, Joe Benjamin, who started the Grimsby playground in 1955 and has been concerned with many such ventures since those days, answered critics in a memorable letter:

> By what criteria are adventure playgrounds to be judged? If it is by the disciplined activity of the uniformed organisations, then there is no doubt but we are a failure. If it is by the success of our football and table tennis teams then there is no doubt we are a flop. If it is by the enterprise and endurance called for by some of the national youth awards – then we must be ashamed.
>
> But these are the standards set by the club movement, in one form or another, for a particular type of child. They do not attract the so-called 'unclubbable', and worse – so we read regularly – nor do they hold those children at whom they are aimed.
>
> May I suggest that we need to examine afresh the pattern taken by the young at play and then compare it with the needs of the growing child and the adolescent. We accept that it is natural for boys and girls below a certain age to play together, and think it equally natural for them to play at being grown up. We accept, in fact, their right to imitate the world around them. Yet as soon as a child is old enough to see through the pretence and demand the reality, we separate him from his sister and try to fob him off with games and activities which seem only to put off the day when he will enter the world proper.
>
> The adventure playgrounds in this country, new though they are, are already providing a number of lessons which we would do well to study … For three successive summers the children have built their dens and created Shanty Town, with its own hospitals, fire station, shops, etc. As each den appeared, it became functional and brought with it an appreciation of its nature and responsibility… The pattern of adventure playgrounds is set by the needs of the children who use them; their 'toys' include woodwork benches and sewing machines… We do not believe that children can be locked up in neat little parcels labelled by age and sex. Neither do we believe that education is the prerogative of the schools.[5]

At the playground he ran at Grimsby there was an annual cycle of growth and renewal. When they began building in the spring, they began with holes in the ground, which gradually gave way to two-storey huts. 'It's the same with fires. They begin by lighting them just for fun. Then they cook potatoes and by the end of the summer they're cooking eggs, bacon and beans.' The ever-changing range of activities was 'due entirely to the imagination and enterprise of the children themselves . . . at no time are they expected to continue an activity which no longer holds an interest for them …'

The adventure playground is a kind of parable of anarchy, a free society in miniature, with the same tensions and ever-changing harmonies, the same diversity and spontaneity, the same unforced growth of co-operation and release of individual qualities and communal sense, which lie dormant in a society whose dominant values are competition and acquisitiveness.

But having discovered something like the ideal conditions for children's play – the self-selected evolution from demolition through discovery to creativity – why should we stop there? Do we really accept the paradox of a free and self-developing childhood followed by a lifetime of dreary and unfulfilling toil? Isn't there a place for the adventure playground or its equivalent in the adult world?

Of course there is, and just as the most striking thing for the visitor, or the organiser, in an adventure playground is not the improvised gymnastics, but the making and building that goes on all around, so the significant thing about adult recreation is not so much the fishing, sailing, pigeon-fancying or photography aspect (though in their organisation these frequently illustrate the principles of self-regulation and free federation that are emphasised in this book), still less is it the commercial and professional sport which is just another aspect of the entertainment industry. The significant aspect is the way in which the urge to make things, and to construct and reconstruct, to repair and remodel, denied outlet in the ordinary sterile world of employment, emerges in the explosion of 'do-it-yourself' activities of every kind.

This in turn leads to a spontaneous sharing of equipment and skills:

> 'I've got two very good friends,' Mrs Jarvis said, 'Mrs Barker, who lives opposite, has got a spin drier and I've got a sewing machine. I put my washing in her spin drier and she uses my sewing machine when she wants to. Then the lady next door on one side is another friend of mine. We always help each other out.' Mr Dover's great hobby is woodwork; at the time he was interviewed he was busy on a pelmet he was making for a friend living next door and he had just finished a toy train for the son of another. He relies on Fred, another friend who is also a neighbour, to help when needed. 'Just today I was sawing a log for the engine of this train and Fred sees that my saw is blunt and lends me a sharp one. Anything at all I want he'll lend it to me if he has it. I'm the same with him. The other day he knocked when I wasn't here and borrowed my steps – we take each other for granted that way.'[6]

The continually increasing scope of the activities people undertake in their spare time is illustrated by the kind of tools and equipment, beyond the range of ordinary sharing between neighbours, that can be hired. One firm which has spread all over the London area hires by the day, week, 'long weekend' and 'short weekend' anything up to mechanical concrete mixers, Kango hammers, scaffolding, industrial spraying plant and welding equipment. Undoubtedly it provides a valuable service, and its overheads must be high, but there is little doubt, from a comparison of its hire charges with the market prices of the equipment, that for many of the hundreds of items which it lets out on hire, joint ownership by a group of neighbours would prove more economical to the individual user.

Take, as another approach, the case of power tools, domestic sales of which have risen phenomenally in the last twenty years. They have grown from the introduction in the 1930s of small portable electric drills in the joinery industry on work which was too large or too unwieldy to be conveniently brought onto fixed machinery. The typical power drills for the amateur market have developed from these machines and from the principle of bringing the tool to the work instead of the work to the machine. They have enormously increased the capabilities of the home handyman, not merely by the reduction of the physical work involved but also by bringing much higher standards of fit and finish within his reach. The basic tool is always the drill and there is now a wide range of specialist attachments. The makers also offer bench fitments to convert the portable tools to bench drills or lathes or saw tables in which the tool is used as a fixed motor. Commenting on this trend, J. Beresford-Evans said:

> At first sight this idea seems admirable, yet it is reactionary in that it denies most of the advantages that the portable tool offers. Most multi-purpose appliances pay for their versatility by a loss of efficiency in each individual job they perform – unless the machine is so designed that the over-all efficiency is great enough to compensate for this loss. But the degree of power, structural strength and precision of manufacture required for such a tool would immediately price it out of the very market at which the makers of amateurs' power tools are aiming.[7]

The way out of this dilemma is again the pooling of equipment in a neighbourhood group. Suppose that each member of the group had a powerful and robust basic tool, while the group as a whole had, for example, a bench drill, lathes and a saw bench to relieve members from the attempt to cope with work which required these machines with inadequate tools of their own, or wasted their resources on under-used individually-owned plant. This in turn demands some kind of building to house the machinery: the Community Workshop.

But is the Community Workshop idea nothing more than an aspect of the leisure industry, a compensation for the tedium of work? Daniel Bell, commenting on the 'fantastic mushrooming of arts-and-crafts hobbies, of photography, home woodwork shops with power-driven tools, ceramics, high fidelity, electronics' notes that this has been achieved at a very high cost indeed – 'the loss of satisfaction in work'.[8] Another American critic presses home this point:

The two worlds of work and leisure drift farther apart. The recreation world contains all the good, bright, pleasant things, and the work world becomes the dreariest place imaginable ... There are certain basic emotional needs that the individual worker must satisfy. To the degree that the ordinary events of the day are not meeting these needs, recreation serves as a sort of mixture of concentrates to supply these missing satisfactions. When the work experience satisfies virtually none of the requirements, the load on recreation becomes impossible.[9]

I want to return to this problem and to the role of the Community Workshop but to consider first the anarchist approach to the organisation of work.

Chapter XI

A SELF-EMPLOYED SOCIETY

The split between life and work is probably the greatest contemporary social problem. You cannot expect men to take a responsible attitude and to display initiative in daily life when their whole working experience deprives them of the chance of initiative and responsibility. The personality cannot be successfully divided into watertight compartments, and even the attempt to do so is dangerous: if a man is taught to rely upon a paternalistic authority within the factory, he will be ready to rely upon one outside. If he is rendered irresponsible at work by lack of opportunity for responsibility, he will be irresponsible when away from work too. The contemporary social trend towards a centralised, paternalistic, authoritarian society only reflects conditions which already exist within the factory.

GORDON RATTRAY TAYLOR, *Are Workers Human?*

The novelist, Nigel Balchin, was once invited to address a conference on 'incentives' in industry. He remarked that 'Industrial psychologists must stop messing about with tricky and ingenious bonus schemes and find out why a man, after a hard day's work, went home and enjoyed digging in his garden.'

But don't we already know why? He enjoys going home and digging in his garden because there he is free from foremen, managers and bosses. He is free from the monotony and slavery of doing the same thing day in day out, and is in control of the whole job from start to finish. He is free to decide for himself how and when to set about it. He is responsible to himself and not to somebody else. He is working because he *wants* to and not because he *has* to. He is doing his own thing. He is his own man.

The desire to 'be your own boss' is very common indeed. Think of all the people whose secret dream or cherished ambition is to run a small-holding or a little shop or to set up in trade on their own account, even though it may mean working night and day with little prospect of solvency. Few of them are such optimists as to think they will make a fortune that way. What they want above all is the sense of independence and of controlling their own destinies.

The fact that in the twentieth century the production and distribution of goods and services is far too complicated to be run by millions of one-man businesses doesn't lessen this urge for self-determination, and the politicians, managers and giant international corporations know it. This is why they present every kind of scheme for 'workers' participation', 'joint management', 'profit sharing', 'industrial co-partnership', everything in fact from suggestion boxes to works councils, to give the worker the *feeling* that he is more than a cog in the industrial machine while making sure that effective control of industry is kept out of the hands of the man on the factory floor. They are in fact like the rich man in Tolstoy's fable – they will do anything for the worker except get off his back.

In every industrial country, and probably in every agricultural country, the idea of workers' control has manifested itself at one time or another – as a demand, an aspiration, a programme or a dream. To confine ourselves to one century and one country, it was the basis of two parallel movements in Britain around the First World War, Syndicalism and Guild Socialism. These two movements dwindled away in the early 1920s, but ever since then there have been sporadic and periodic attempts to re-create a movement for workers' control of industry. From some points of view the advocates of workers' control had much more reason for optimism in 1920 than today. In that year the Sankey Report (a majority report of a Royal Commission) advocating 'joint control' and public ownership of the mining industry in Britain, was turned down by the government for being too radical, and by the shop stewards for not being radical enough. When the mines were actually nationalised after almost thirty years, nothing even as mild as joint control was either proposed or demanded. In 1920, too, the Building Guilds began their brief but successful existence. In our own day it is inconceivable that large local authorities would let big building contracts to guilds of workers, or that the co-operative movement would finance them. The idea that workers should have some say in the running of their industries was accepted then in a way that it has never been since.

And yet the trade union movement today is immeasurably stronger than it was in the days when workers' control was a widespread demand. What has happened is that the labour movement as a whole has accepted the notion that you gain more by settling for less. In most Western countries, as Anthony Crosland pointed out, the unions, 'greatly aided by propitious changes in the political and economic background, have achieved a more effective control through the independent exercise of their collective bargaining strength than they would ever have achieved by following the path (beset as it is by practical difficulties on which all past experiments have foundered) of direct workers' management. Indeed we may risk the generalisation that the greater the power of the unions the less the interest in workers' management.'[1]

His observation is true, even if it is unpalatable for those who would like to see the unions, or some more militantly syndicalist kind of industrial union, as the vehicle for workers' control. Many advocates of workers' control have seen the unions as the organs through which it is to be exercised, assuming presumably that the attainment of workers' control would bring complete community of interest in industry and that the defensive role of the unions would become obsolete. (This is, of course, the assumption behind trade union organisation in the Soviet empire). I think this view is a gross over-simplification. Before the First World War, the Webbs pointed out that 'the decisions of the most democratically elected executive committees with regard to wages, hours and conditions of employment of particular sections of their fellow workers, do not always satisfy the latter, or even seem to them to be just'. And the Yugoslav scholar, Branko Pribicević, in his history of the shop-stewards' movement in Britain, emphasises this point in criticising the reliance on the idea of control by industrial unions:

> Control of industry is largely incompatible with a union's character as a voluntary association of the workers, formed primarily to protect and represent their interests. Even in the most democratic industrial system, i.e. a system in which the workers would have a share in control, there would still be a need for unions ... Now if we assume that managers would be responsible to the body of workers, we cannot exclude the possibility of individual injustices and mistakes. Such cases must be taken up by the union ... It seems most improbable that a union could fulfil any of these tasks successfully if it were also the organ of industrial administration or, in other words, if it had ceased to be a voluntary organisation ...
>
> It was unfortunate that the idea of workers' control was almost completely identified with the concept of union control ... It was obvious throughout that the unions would oppose any doctrine aiming at creating a representative structure in industry parallel with their own.[2]

In fact, in the only instances we know of in Britain, of either complete or partial workers' control, the trade union structure is entirely separate from the administration, and there has never been any suggestion that it should be otherwise. What are these examples? Well, there are the co-operative co-partnerships which make, for instance, some of the footware sold in retail co-operative societies. These are, so far as they go, genuine examples of workers' control (needless to say I am not speaking of the factories run by the Cooperative Wholesale Society on orthodox capitalist lines), but they do not seem to have any capacity for expansion, or to exercise any influence on industry in general. There are the fishermen of Brixham in Devon, and the miners of Brora on the coast of Sutherland in Scotland. This pit was to have shut down, but instead the miners took it over from the National Coal Board and formed a company of their own. Then there are those firms where some form of control by the employees has been sought by idealistic employers. (I am thinking of firms like Scott Bader Ltd., and Farmer and Co., not of those heavily paternalistic chocolate manufacturers or of spurious co-partnerships). There are also odd small workshops like the factories in Scotland and Wales of the Rowen Engineering Company.

I mention these examples, not because they have any economic significance, but because the general view is that control of industry by workers is a beautiful idea which is utterly impracticable because of some unspecified deficiency, not in the idea, but in those people labelled as 'workers'. The Labour Correspondent of *The Times* remarked of ventures of this kind that, while they provide 'a means of harmonious self-government in a small concern', there is no evidence that they provide 'any solution to the problem of establishing democracy in large-scale industry'. And even more widespread than the opinion that workers have a built-in capacity for managing themselves, is the regretful conclusion that workers' control is a nice idea, but one which is totally incapable of realisation because of the scale and complexity of modern industry. Daniel Guérin recommends an interpretation of anarchism which 'rests upon large-scale modern industry, up-to-date techniques, the modern proletariat, and internationalism on a world scale'. But he does not tell us how. On the face of it, we could counter the argument about scope and scale by pointing out how changes in sources of motive power make the geographical concentration of industry obsolete, and how changing methods of production (automation for example) make the concentration of vast numbers of people obsolete too. Decentralisation is perfectly feasible, and probably economically advantageous within the structure of industry as it is today. But the arguments based on the complexity of modern industry actually mean something quite different.

What the sceptics really mean is that while they can imagine the isolated case of a small enterprise in which the shares are held by the employees, but which is run on ordinary business lines – like Scott Bader Ltd. – or while they can accept the odd example of a firm in which a management committee is elected by the workers – like the co-operative co-partnerships – they cannot imagine those who manipulate the commanding heights of the economy being either disturbed by or, least of all, influenced by, these admirable small-scale precedents. And they are right, of course: the minority aspiration for workers' control which never completely dies, has at the same time never been widespread enough to challenge the controllers of industry, in spite of the ideological implications of the 'work-in'.

The tiny minority who would like to see revolutionary changes need not cherish any illusions about this. Neither in the political parties of the Left nor in the trade union movement will they find more than a similar minority in agreement. Nor does the history of syndicalist movements in any country, even Spain, give them any cause for optimism. Geoffrey Ostergaard puts their dilemma in these terms: 'To be effective as defensive organisations, the unions needed to embrace as many workers as possible and this inevitably led to a dilution of their revolutionary objectives. In practice, the syndicalists were faced with the choice of unions which were *either* reformist and purely defensive *or* revolutionary and largely ineffective.'[3]

Is there a way out of this dilemma? An approach which combines the ordinary day-to-day struggle of workers in industry over wages and conditions with a more radical attempt to shift the balance of power in the factory? I believe that there is, in what the syndicalists and guild socialists used to describe as 'encroaching control' by means of the 'collective contract'. The syndicalists saw this as 'a system by which the workers within a factory or shop would undertake a specific amount of work in return for a lump sum to be allocated by the work-group as it saw fit, on condition that the employers abdicated their control of the productive process itself'. The late G. D. H. Cole, who returned to the advocacy of the collective contract system towards the end of his life, claimed that 'the effect would be to link the members of the working group together in a common enterprise under their joint auspices and control, and to emancipate them from an externally imposed discipline in respect of their method of getting the work done'. I believe that it has, and my evidence for this belief comes from the example of the gang system worked in some Coventry factories which has some aspects in common with the collective contract idea, and the 'Composite work' system worked in some Durham coal mines, which has everything in common with it.

The first of these, the gang system, was described by an American professor of industrial and management engineering, Seymour Melman, in his book *Decision-Making and Productivity*, where he sought 'to demonstrate that there are realistic alternatives to managerial rule over production'. I have been publicising this book for years simply because in all the pretentious drivel of industrial management literature (which may not fool the workers, but certainly fools management) it is the only piece of research I have come across which raises the key question: is management necessary? Melman sought out an identical product made under dissimilar conditions, and found it in the Ferguson tractor made

under licence in both Detroit and Coventry. His account of the operation of the gang system in Coventry was confirmed for me by a
Coventry engineering worker, Reg Wright.

Of Standard's tractor factory (he is writing of the period before
Standard sold the plant to Massey-Ferguson in 1956, and before Leyland
took over Standard), Melman declares, 'In this firm we will show that at
the same time thousands of workers operated virtually without supervision as conventionally understood, and at high productivity: the highest
wage in British industry was paid; high quality products were produced
at acceptable prices in extensively mechanised plants; the management
conducted its affairs at unusually low costs; also, organised workers had a
substantial role in production decision-making.' The production policy
of the firm at that time was most unorthodox for the motor industry and
was the resultant of two inter-related decision-making systems, that of
the workers and that of management: 'In production, the management
has been prepared to pay a high wage and to organise production via the
gang system which requires management to deal with a grouped work
force, rather than with single workers, or with small groups ... the
foremen are concerned with the detailed surveillance of things rather
than with the detailed control over people ... The operation of inte-
grated plants employing 10,000 production workers did not require the
elaborate and costly hallmark of business management.'[4]

In the motor-car factory fifteen gangs ranged in size from fifty to five
hundred people and the tractor factory was organised as one huge gang.
From the standpoint of the production workers 'the gang system leads to
keeping track of goods instead of keeping track of people'. For payment
purposes the output that was measured was the output of the whole
group. In relation to management, Melman points out: 'The grouped
voice of a work force had greater impact than the pressure of single
workers. This effect of the gang system, coupled with trade unionism, is
well understood among many British managements. As a result, many
managements have opposed the use of the gang system and have argued
the value of single worker incentive payments.

In a telling comparison, Melman contrasts the 'predatory competition' which characterises the managerial decision-making system with
the workers' decision-making system in which 'The most characteristic
feature of the decision-formulating process is that of *mutuality* in
decision-making with final authority residing in the hands of the
grouped workers themselves.'

Emphasising the *human* significance of this mode of industrial organisation, Reg Wright says:

> The gang system sets men's minds free from many worries and enables
> them to concentrate completely on the job. It provides a natural frame

99

of security, it gives confidence, shares money equally, uses all degrees of skill without distinction and enables jobs to be allocated to the man or woman best suited to them, the allocation frequently being made by the workers themselves. Change of job to avoid monotony is an easy matter. The 'gaffer' is abolished and foremen are now technicians called in to advise, or to act in a breakdown or other emergency. In some firms a *ganger* will run, not the men, but the *job*. He will be paid out of gang earnings, and will work himself on a small gang. On a larger gang he will be fully occupied with organisation and supply of parts and materials. A larger gang may have a deputy ganger as a second string and also a *gang-steward* who, being a keen trade unionist or workers' man, will act as a corrective should the gangers try to favour management unduly or interfere with the individual in undesirable ways. Gang meetings are called as necessary, by the latter and all members of the gang are kept informed and may (and do) criticise everything and everybody. All three are subject to recall. Constructive ideas, on the other hand, are usually the result of one or two people thinking out and trying out new things – this is taking place continuously ...[5]

He remarks that 'The fact of taking responsibility in any of these capacities is *educative* in every sense.' Certainly the usual methods of work organisation are not only divisive ('They'd cut your throat for a bit more overtime,' a Ford worker told Graham Turner) but are profoundly *de-educative*, reducing the worker, as Eric Gill used to put it, to a 'subhuman condition of intellectual irresponsibility'.

My second example comes from the mining industry in Durham. David Douglass in his book *Pit Life in County Durham*, criticises the attempts of the National Coal Board to introduce more and more supervision into the miner's work, with the intention of working the mines like factories, remarking that 'one of the few redeeming features of pit work, and one that the miners will fight to maintain, is that of independent job control', for while 'most factory workers would regard the mine purely and simply as a black and filthy hole, funnily enough the miner in turn regards the factory as a prison and its operatives as captives'. In the early days of mining in Durham, he explains, 'the miner was practically a self-governing agent. The hewers were allowed to manage their own jobs with practically a total lack of supervision. The degree of job control (though necessarily limited by private ownership) was almost complete.' Douglass describes such traditions as the *cavilling* system (selection of working-place by ballot in order to equalise earning opportunities) as:

the fundamental way in which the Durham miner managed to maintain an equitable system of work, and managed to stave off the competitiveness, bullying and injustice of the hated butty system. In essence it was an embryo of workers' control, as can be seen from its ability to handle disputes between sets of workers without recourse to outsiders. It was a little Soviet which had grown up within the capitalist system. In a sense it was of necessity restricted in its development. It is, however, a feature of the worker intervening in the productive process in a conscious way to say: this is how I run it, you adapt it accordingly.[6]

The same kind of attempt to run the mines as factories that David Douglass complains of, accompanied the introduction in the post-war years of the 'long-wall' system of working. A comparative study was made by the Tavistock Institute of conventional long-wall working with its introduction of the division of labour, and of factory-type methods, and the composite long-wall method adopted by the miners in some pits. Its importance for my argument can be seen from the opening words of one of the Tavistock reports:

> This study concerns a groups of miners who came together to evolve a new way of working together, planning the type of change they wanted to put through, and testing it in practice. The new type of work organisation which has come to be known in the industry as composite working, has in recent years emerged spontaneously in a number of different pits in the north-west Durham coalfield. Its roots go back to an earlier tradition which has been almost completely displaced in the course of the last century by the introduction of work techniques based on task segmentation, differential status and payment, and extrinsic hierarchical control.[7]

A further report notes how the investigation shows 'the ability of quite large primary work groups of 40-50 members to act as self-regulating, self-developing social organisms able to maintain themselves in a steady state of high productivity ...'[8] P. G. Herbst describes the system of composite working in a way which shows its relationship to the gang system:

> The composite work organisation may be described as one in which the group takes over complete responsibility for the total cycle of operations involved in mining the coal face. No member of the group has a fixed work-role. Instead, the men deploy themselves, depending on the requirements of the ongoing group task. Within the limits of technological and safety requirements they are free to evolve their own way of organising and carrying out their task. They are not subject to any external authority in this respect, nor is there within the group itself any member who takes over a formal directive leadership function. Whereas in conventional long-wall working the coal-getting task is split into four

or eight separate work roles, carried out by different teams, each paid at a different rate, in the composite group members are no longer paid directly for any of the tasks carried out. The all-in wage agreement is, instead, based on the negotiated price per ton of coal produced by the team. The income obtained is divided equally among team members.[9]

These examples of on-the-job workers' control are important in evolving an anarchist approach to industrial organisation. They do not entail submission to paternalistic management techniques – in fact they demolish the myths of managerial expertise and indispensability. They are a force for solidarity rather than divisiveness between workers on the basis of pay and status. They illustrate that it is possible to bring decision-making back to the factory floor and the face-to-face group. They even satisfy – though this is not my criterion for recommending them – the capitalist test of productivity. They, like the growing concept of workers' rights of *possession* in the job – tacitly recognised in redundancy payment legislation, actively demonstrated by workers taking over physical possession of the workplace as in the 'work-in' at Upper Clyde Shipbuilders – have the great tactical merit of combining short-term aims with long-term aspirations.

Could the workers run industry? Of course they could. They do already. Neither of the two examples I have given of successful 'on the job' control, exists in the same form today, for reasons which have nothing to do with either their efficiency or their productivity. In the Durham example it has to do with the shift of emphasis in the (publicly-owned) National Coal Board to the coalfields of South Yorkshire and Nottingham, and in the case of Standards with the mergers (sponsored by a Labour government) which led to the formation of British Leyland as a combine large enough to compete for markets with the giant American-owned and European firms.

Industry is not dominated by technical expertise, but by the sales manager, the accountant and the financial tycoon who never made anything in their lives except money.

For a lucky few work is enjoyable for its own sake, but the proportion of such people in the total working population grows smaller as work becomes either more mechanised or more fragmented. Automation, which was expected to reduce the sheer drudgery of manual labour and the sheer mental drudgery of clerical work, is feared because in practice it simply reduces the number of income-gaining opportunities. It is a saving of labour, not by the worker, but by the owners or controllers of capital. The lucky few are destined for the jobs which are either created by or are unaffected by automation. The unlucky majority, condemned from childhood to the dreary jobs, find them either diminished or extinguished by the 'rationalisation' of work.

Can we imagine that in a situation where the control of an industry, a factory, any kind of workplace, was in the hands of the people who work there, they would just carry on production, distribution and bottle-washing in the ways we are familiar with today? Even within capitalist society (though not within the 'public sector' which belongs to 'the people') some employers find that what they call job enlargement or job enrichment, the replacement of conveyor belt tasks by complete assembly jobs, or deliberate rotation from job to job in the production process can increase production simply by reducing boredom. When everyone in an industry has a voice in it, would they stop at this point?

In his brilliant essay *Work and Surplus*, Keith Paton imagines what would happen in a car factory taken over permanently by its workers. 'After the carnival of revolution come the appeals to return to work' but 'to get into the habit of responding to orders or exhortations to raise the GNP would be to sell the pass straight away. On the other hand production must eventually be got going on *some* basis or other. What basis? Return to *what sort of work*?'

> So instead of restarting the assembly track (if the young workers haven't already smashed it) they spend two months discussing the point of their work, and how to rearrange it. Private cars? Why do people always want to go somewhere else? Is it because where they are is so intolerable? And what part did the automobile play in making the need to escape? What about day to day convenience? Is being stuck in a traffic jam convenient? What about the cost to the country? Bugger the 'cost to the country', that's just the same crap as the national interest. Have you seen the faces of old people as they try to cross a busy main road? What about the inconvenience to pedestrians? What's the reason for buying a car? Is it just wanting to HAVE it? Do we think the value of a car rubs off on us? But that's the wrong way round. Does having a car really save time? What's the average hours worked in manufacturing industry? Let's look it up in the library: 45.7 hours work a week. What's the amount of the family's spending money in a week that goes on cars? 10.3 per cent of all family income. Which means more like 20 per cent if you've got a car because half of us don't have one. What's 25 per cent of 45 hours? Christ, 9 hours! That's a hell of a long time spent 'saving time'! There must be a better way of getting from A to B. By bus? OK, let's make buses. But what about the pollution and that? What about those electric cars they showed on the telly once? Etc., etc.[10]

He envisages another month of discussion and research in complexly cross-cutting groups, until the workers reach a consensus for eventual self-redeployment for making products which the workers consider to be socially useful. These include car refurbishing (to increase the use-value of models already on the road), buses, overhead monorail cars, electric cars and scooters, white bicycles for communal use (as devised by the Amsterdam provos), housing units, minimal work for drop-outs, and for kids and old people who like to make themselves useful. But he sees other aspects of the workers' take-over, voluntary extra work for example: 'As work becomes more and more pleasurable, as technology and society develop to allow more and more craft aspects to return at high technological level, the idea of *voluntary extra* over the (reduced) fixed working week becomes feasible. Even the fixing of the working week becomes superseded.' The purpose of this voluntary extra? 'New Delhi needs buses, provide them by voluntary work.'[11]

The factory itself is open to the community, including children; 'thus every factory worker is a potential "environmental studies" instructor, if a child comes up and asks him how something works.' The factory in fact becomes a university, an institute of learning rather than of enforced stupidity, 'using men to a millionth of their capacities' as Norbert Weiner put it.

The evolution and transformation of the factory envisaged by Keith Paton leads us back to the idea of the Community Workshop envisaged in the previous chapter. We tend to think of the motor industry, for example, as one in which iron ore comes in at one end and a complete car rolls out at the other (though the purchaser of a 'Friday car' in today's society had better watch out, for that car rolled off the assembly line when the workers were waiting for their real life at the weekend to begin). But in fact two thirds of the factory value of a car is represented by components bought by the manufacturers from outside suppliers. The motor industry, like many others, is an *assembly* industry. The fact that this is so of most consumer goods industries, coupled with the modern facts of widely distributed industrial skill and motive power, means that, as the Goodman brothers said in *Communitas:* 'In large areas of our operation, we could go back to old-fashioned domestic industry with perhaps even a gain in efficiency, for small power is everywhere available, small machines are cheap and ingenious, and there are easy means to collect machined parts and centrally assemble them.'[12] But it also means that we could *locally* assemble them. It already happens on the individual spare-time level. Build-it-yourself radio, record-playing, and television kits are a commonplace, and you can also buy assemble-it-yourself cars and refrigerators.

Groups of community workshops could combine for bulk ordering of components, or for sharing according to their capacity the production of components for mutual exchange and for local assembly. The new industrial field of plastics (assuming that in a transformed future society, people find it a genuine economy to use them) offer many unexploited possibilities for the community workshop. There are three main kinds of plastics today: thermosetting resins which are moulded under heat with very high pressures and consequently require plant which is at present expensive and complex; thermoplastics, which are shaped by extrusion and by injection moulding (there are already do-it-yourself electric thermoplastic injection machines on the market); and polyester resins, used in conjunction with reinforcing materials like glass fibre which can be moulded at low pressures by simple contact moulding, and are thus eminently suitable for the potentialities of the community workshop.

As we are frequently reminded by our own experience as consumers, industrial products in our society are built for a limited life as well as for an early obsolescence. The products which are available for purchase are not the products which we would prefer to have. In a worker-controlled society it would not be worth the workers' while to produce articles with a deliberately limited life, nor to make things which were unrepairable. Products would have *transparency of operation and repair*. When Henry Ford first marketed his Model T he aimed at a product which 'any hick up a dirt road' could repair with a hammer and a spanner. He nearly bankrupted his firm in the process, but this is precisely the kind of product which an anarchist society would need: objects whose functioning is transparent and whose repair can be undertaken readily and simply by the user.

In his book *The Worker in an Affluent Society*, Ferdynand Zweig makes the entertaining observation that 'quite often the worker comes to work on Monday worn out from his weekend activities, especially from "Do-it-yourself"'. Quite a number said that the weekend is the most trying and exacting period of the whole week, and Monday morning in the factory, in comparison, is relaxing.'[13] This leads us to ask – not in the future, but in our present society – what *is* work and what *is* leisure if we work harder in our leisure than at our work? The fact that one of these jobs is paid and the other is not seems almost fortuitous. And this in turn leads us to a further question. The paradoxes of contemporary capitalism mean that there are vast numbers of what one American economist calls *no-people*: the army of the unemployed who are either unwanted by, or who consciously reject, the meaningless mechanised slavery of contemporary industrial production. Could they make a livelihood for themselves today in the community workshop? If the workshop is conceived merely as a social service for 'creative leisure' the answer is that it would probably be against the rules. Members might complain that so-and-so was abusing the facilities provided by using them 'commercially'. But if the workshop were conceived on more imaginative lines than any existing venture of this kind, its potentialities could become a source of livelihood in the truest sense. In several of the New Towns in Britain, for example, it has been found necessary and desirable to build groups of small workshops for individuals and small businesses engaged in such work as repairing electrical equipment or car bodies, woodworking and

105

the manufacture of small components. The Community Workshop would be enhanced by its cluster of separate workplaces for 'gainful' work. Couldn't the workshop become the community *factory*, providing work or a place for work for anyone in the locality who wanted to work that way, not as an optional extra to the economy of the affluent society which rejects an increasing proportion of its members, but as one of the prerequisites of the worker-controlled economy of the future?

Keith Paton again, in a far-sighted pamphlet addressed to members of the Claimants' Union, urged them not to compete for meaningless jobs in the economy which has thrown them out as redundant, but to use their skills to serve their own community. (One of the characteristics of the affluent world is that it denies its poor the opportunity to feed, clothe, or house *themselves*, or to meet their own and their families' needs, except from grudgingly doled-out welfare payments). He explains that:

> When we talk of 'doing our own thing' we are not advocating going back to doing everything by hand. This would have been the only option in the thirties. But since then electrical power and 'affluence' have brought a spread of *intermediate* machines, some of them very sophisticated, to ordinary working class communities. Even if they do not own them (as many claimants do not) the possibility exists of borrowing them from neighbours, relatives, ex-workmates. Knitting and sewing machines, power tools and other do-it-yourself equipment comes in this category. Garages can be converted into little workshops, home-brew kits are popular, parts and machinery can be taken from old cars and other gadgets. If they saw their opportunity, trained metallurgists and mechanics could get into advanced scrap technology, recycling the metal wastes of the consumer society for things which could be used again regardless of whether they would fetch anything in a shop. Many hobby enthusiasts could begin to see their interests in a new light.[14]

'We do', he affirms, '*need* each other and the enormous pool of energy and morale that lies untapped in every ghetto, city district and estate.' The funny thing is that when we discuss the question of work from an anarchist point of view, the first question people ask is: What would you do about the lazy man, the man who will not work? The only possible answer is that we have all been supporting him for centuries. The problem that faces every individual and every society is quite different, it is how to provide people with the opportunity they yearn for: the chance to be useful.

Chapter XII

THE BREAKDOWN OF WELFARE

All institutions, all social organisations, impose a pattern on people and detract from their individuality; above all it seems to me, they detract from their humanity . . . It seems to me that one thing is in the nature of all institutions, whether they are for good purposes, like colleges, schools and hospitals, or for evil purposes, like prisons. Everyone in an institution is continually adapting himself to it, and to other people, whereas the glory of humanity is that it adapts its environment to mankind, not human beings to their environment.

JOHN VAIZEY, *Scenes from Institutional Life*

Anarchists are sometimes told that their simple picture of the state as the protector of the privileges of the powerful is hopelessly out of date: welfare has changed the state. Some politicians even claim that their parties invented welfare. The late Hugh Gaitskill, for instance, described the welfare state as 'another Labour achievement', adding that 'unfortunately gratitude is not a reliable political asset'. In fact the candidates for office in most Western governments rival each other in the welfare packages they offer the electorate.

But what do we mean by the welfare state? Social welfare can exist without the state. States can, and frequently do, exist without undertaking responsibility for social welfare. Every kind of human association may be a welfare society: trade unions, Christmas clubs, churches and teenage gangs – all of which presumably aim at mutual benefit, comfort and security – can be considered as aspects of social welfare. The state, as we have seen, is a form of social organisation which differs from all the rest in two respects: firstly, that it claims the allegiance of the whole population rather than those who have opted to join it, and secondly, that it has coercive power to enforce that allegiance. Association for mutual welfare is as old as humanity – we wouldn't be here if it were not – and is biological in origin. Kropotkin, whose *Mutual Aid* chronicles

107

this innate human tendency, describes, not the strengthening, but the destruction of the social institutions that embodied it, with the growth of the modern European nation-state from the fifteenth century onward:

> For the next three centuries the States, both on the continent and in these islands, systematically weeded out all institutions in which the mutual aid tendency had formerly found its expression. The village communities were bereft of their folkmotes, their courts and independent administration: their lands were confiscated. The guilds were spoilated of their possessions and liberties, and placed under the control, the fancy, and the bribery of the State's official. The cities were divested of their sovereignty, and the very springs of their inner life – the folkmote, the elected justices and their administration, the sovereign parish and the sovereign guild – were annihilated; the State's functionary took possession of every link of what was formerly an organic whole ... It was taught in the universities and from the pulpit that the institutions in which men formerly used to embody their needs of mutual support could not be tolerated in a properly organised State; that the state alone could represent the bonds of union between its subjects; that federalism and 'particularism' were the enemies of progress, and the State was the only proper initiator of further development.[1]

This is not an old-fashioned romantic view of the passing of the Middle Ages: it is reflected in modern scholarship, for example in Ullmann's *Government and People in the Middle Ages.* Nor is Kropotkin's bitter account of it exaggerated, as you can see from the history of pauperism in Britain. In the Middle Ages destitution was relieved without recourse to state action. Guild members who fell into poverty were assisted by the fraternity, whose concern extended to their widows and orphans. There were hospitals and lazar-houses for the sick, and monastic hospitality was extended to all who needed it. But with the establishment of a firmly based nation-state by the Tudors, it was characteristic that the first state legislation on poverty required that beggars should be whipped and that the second required that they should be branded, and that the essence of the Poor Law from its codification in 1601 to its amendment in 1834 and its final disappearance in our own time, was punitive. Any member of the Claimants' Union today would insist that the Poor Law *still* exists and that it *is* punitive.

We may thus conclude that there is an essential paradox in the fact that the state whose symbols are the policeman, the jailer and the soldier should have become the administrator and organiser of social welfare. The connection between welfare and warfare is in fact very close. Until late in the nineteenth century the state conducted its wars with professional soldiers and mercenaries, but the increasing scale and scope of wars forced states to pay more and more attention to the physical quality of recruits, whether volunteers or conscripts, and the discovery that so large a proportion of the eligible cannon-fodder was physically unfit (a discovery it has made afresh with every war of the last hundred years) led the state to take measures for improving the physical health of the nation. Richard Titmuss remarks in his essay on *War and Social Policy* that 'It was the South African War, not one of the notable wars in human history to change the affairs of men, that touched off the personal health movement which eventually led to the National Health Service in 1948.'[2]

With the extension of warfare to the civilian population, the need to maintain morale by the formulation of 'peace aims' and the general feeling of guilt over past social injustices and of resolution to do better in future which war engenders, the concern over physical health extended to a wider field of social well-being. The 'wartime trends towards universalising public provision for certain basic needs', as Titmuss says, 'mean in effect that a social system must be so organised as to enable all citizens (and not only soldiers) to learn what to make of their lives in peacetime. In this context, the Education Act of 1944 becomes intelligible; so does the Beveridge Report of 1942 and the National Insurance, Family Allowances and National Service Acts. All these measures of social policy were in part an expression of the needs of war-time strategy to fuse and unify the conditions of life of civilians and non-civilians alike.'[3]

His sardonic conclusion is that 'The aims and content of social policy, both in peace and war, are thus determined – at least to a substantial extent – by how far the co-operation of the masses is essential to the successful prosecution of war.'

There are in fact several quite separate traditions of social welfare: the product of totally different attitudes to social needs. Even in the unified provision under the state's welfare legislation these traditions live on. A friend of mine, an experimental psychologist who visits many hospitals, says that although it is several decades since the establishment of the National Health Service, he can always tell whether a particular institution grew out of a voluntary hospital, a municipal one, or a Poor Law institution. One of these traditions is that of a service given grudgingly and punitively by authority, another is the expression of social responsibility, or of mutual aid and self-help. One is embodied in *institutions,* the other in *associations.*

In the jargon of social administration there is an ugly but expressive word 'institutionalisation', meaning putting people into institutions. There is also an even uglier word, 'de-institutionalisation', meaning getting them out again. Regrettable the word may be, but it describes a trend that is profoundly significant from an anarchist point of view. 'Institution' in a general sense means 'an established law, custom, usage, practice, organisation, or other element in the political or social life of a people' and in a special sense means 'an educational, philanthropic, remedial, or penal establishment in which a building or system of buildings plays a major and central role, *e.g.* schools, hospitals, orphanages, old people's homes, jails'. If you accept these definitions you will see that anarchism is hostile to institutions in the general sense, hostile, that is to say, to the institutionalisation into pre-established forms or legal entities of the various kinds of human association. It is predisposed towards de-institutionalisation, towards the breakdown of institutions.

Now de-institutionalisation is a feature of current thought and actual trends in the second or special sense of the word. There is a characteristic pattern of development common to many of these special institutions. Frequently they were founded or modified by some individual pioneer, a secular or religious philanthropist, to meet some urgent social need, or remedy some social evil. Then they became the focus of the activities of a voluntary society, and as the nineteenth century proceeded, gained the acknowledgement and support of the state. Local authorities filled in the geographical gaps in their distribution and finally, in our own century, the institutions themselves have been institutionalised, that is to say nationalised, or taken over by the state as a public service.

But at the very peak of their growth and development a doubt has arisen. Are they in fact remedying the evil or serving the purpose for which they were instituted, or are they merely perpetuating it? A new generation of pioneer thinkers arises which seeks to set the process in reverse, to abolish the institution altogether, or to break it down into non-institutional units, or to meet the same social need in a non-institutional way. This is so marked a trend that it leads us to speculate on the extent to which the special institutions can be regarded as microcosms or models for the critical examination of the general institutions of society.

In one sense the institutions found their architectural expression in a hierarchy of huge Victorian buildings in the cemetery belt on the fringe of the cities. 'Conveniently adjacent to the cemetery', wrote C. F. Masterman, 'was the immense fever hospital ... In front was a gigantic workhouse; behind a gigantic lunatic asylum; to the right, a gigantic barrack school; to the left, a gigantic prison ... Around the city's borders are studded the gigantic buildings, prisons or palaces which witness to its efforts to grapple with the problems of maimed and distorted life – witness both to its energy and its failure. The broken, the rebellious, the lunatic, the deserted children, the deserted old, are cooped up behind high gates and polished walls.'[4] Heather Woolmer commented: 'Masterman sees these features as a deliberate rejection by society of all it wished to forget, like death, and all which it found inconvenient, like the destitute, old, or mad. It was almost as though an entire sub-culture could be processed on the city fringe: from charity school to workhouse, to old people's institution to hospital to graveyard: like battery chickens awaiting the conveyor belt to death.'[5]

And indeed institutionalisation is a cradle-to-grave affair. A generation ago the accepted 'ideal' pattern of childbirth was in a maternity hospital. The baby was taken away from the mother at birth and put behind glass by a masked nurse, to be brought out at strictly regulated hours for feeding. Kissing and cuddling were regarded as unhygienic. (Most babies were not born that way, but that was the ideal.) Today the ideal picture is completely different. Baby is born at home with father helping the midwife, while brothers and sisters are encouraged to 'share' the new acquisition. He is cossetted by all and sundry and fed on demand. (Again most babies are not born that way, but it is the accepted ideal.) This change in attitudes can be attributed to the swing of the pendulum of fashion, or to common sense re-asserting itself, or to the immensely influential evidence gathered by John Bowlby in his W.H.O. report on maternal care.[6] Ashley Montagu writes:

> there was a disease from which, but half a century ago, more than half of the children [who died] in the first year of life, regularly died. This disease was known as *marasmus* from the Greek word meaning 'wasting away'. This disease was also known as infantile atrophy or debility. When studies were undertaken to track down its cause, it was discovered that it was generally babies in the 'best' homes and hospitals who were most often its victims, babies who were apparently receiving the best and most careful physical attention, while babies in the poorest homes, with a good mother, despite the lack of hygienic physical conditions, often overcame the physical handicaps and flourished. What was lacking in the sterilised environment of the babies of the first class and was generously supplied in the babies of the second class was mother love. This discovery is responsible for the fact that hospitals today endeavour to keep the infant for as short a time as possible.[7]

The conflict between these two 'ideal' patterns of childbirth is still frequently debated. It was reported, for example, that 'Many mothers compare their reception and management in hospital unfavourably with confinement at home. Of one series of 336 mothers who had at least one baby in hospital and one at home, 80 per cent preferred home confinement and only 14 per cent hospital confinement.'[8] This simply means of course that mothers want the advantages of both 'ideals' – medical safety and a domestic atmosphere. The real demand is in fact for the de-institutionalisation of the hospital. Thus when he opened the obstetric unit of Charing Cross Hospital, Professor Norman Morris declared that 'Twenty-five years of achievement have vastly reduced the hazards of childbirth, but hospitals too often drown the joys of motherhood in a sea of inhumanity.' There was, he said, 'an atmosphere of

111

coldness, unfriendliness, and severity, more in keeping with an income tax office. Many of our systems which involve dragooning and regimentation must be completely revised.'[9] Later he described many existing maternity units as mere baby factories. 'Some even seem to boast that they have developed a more efficient conveyor belt system than anything that has gone before.'[10]

The widespread acceptance of the view which has become known as Bowlby's maternal deprivation hypothesis has profoundly affected attitudes to the treatment of young children in hospital. The American paediatricians observed that residence in hospital manifests itself by a fairly well-defined clinical picture. 'A striking feature is the failure to gain properly, despite the ingestion of diets that are entirely adequate for growth in the home. Infants in hospitals sleep less than others and they rarely smile or babble spontaneously. They are listless and apathetic and look unhappy.' Bowlby notes the same thing and remarks that the condition of these infants is 'undoubtedly a form of depression having many of the hallmarks of the typical adult depressive patient of the mental hospital'.[11]

The observations of the effect of the institutional environment on sick children are also true of physically healthy children. One of the first comparative studies of orphanage children with a matched control group led the observers to remark:

> No one could have predicted, much less proved, the steady tendency to deteriorate on the part of children maintained under what had previously been regarded as standard orphanage conditions. With respect to intelligence, vocabulary, general information, social competence, personal adjustment, and motor achievement, the whole picture was one of retardation. The effect of one to three years in a nursery school still far below its own potentialities, was to reverse the tide of regression, which, for some, led to feeble-mindedness.[12]

In Britain during the war Dorothy Burlingham and Anna Freud reported in *Infants Without Families* the striking changes in children showing every sign of retardation when their residential nurseries were broken down to provide family groups of four children each with their own substitute mother, and since then a great number of comparisons have been made in several countries, with results which Barbara Wootton summed up in these words: 'Repeatedly these children have been found to lag behind the standards of those who live at home; to have both lower intelligence and lower developmental quotients, and to be, moreover, relatively backward in both speech and walking ... They were also more destructive and aggressive, more restless and less able to concentrate and more indifferent to privacy rights than other children. They were, in fact, impoverished in all aspects of their personality.'[13] The change in public and official opinion in Britain began with a letter to *The Times* in 1944 from Lady Allen of Hurtwood, who followed it with a pamphlet drawing attention to the grossly unsatisfactory conditions in children's homes and orphanages, giving examples of unimaginative and cruel treatment. As a result a committee was set up in the following year and its report (the Curtis Report on the Care of Children) was issued in December 1946 severely criticising the institutional care of children and making recommendations that have been so widely accepted since that Bowlby was able to write that 'The controversy over the merits of foster-homes and of institutional care can now be regarded as settled. There is now no-one who advocates the care of children in large groups – indeed all advise strongly against it.'

It is not surprising that the methods and attitudes that have proved most successful in de-institutionalising the treatment of normal children and 'normally' sick children should be even more striking with children afflicted in some way, for example spastic or epileptic children, and with mentally handicapped children. In the research project undertaken at Brooklands, Reigate by Dr J. Tizard and Miss Daly, a group of sixteen 'imbecile' children were matched with a control group at the parent hospital. Even after the first year the children cared for on 'family' lines gained an average of eight months in mental age on a verbal intelligence test as against three months for the control group. In personal independence, measured on an age scale, they had increased by six months as against three in the control group, and there were significant developments in speech, social and emotional behaviour and self-chosen activity. Similar experiences of the benefits of small, permissive, family groups have rewarded those who have sought to de-institutionalise the residential care of 'delinquent' or maladjusted children – George Lyward at Finchden Manor, or David Wills at Bodenham, for example.

For many generations the word 'institution' meant, to the majority of people in Britain, one thing, *the* Institution, the Poor Law Infirmary or Union Workhouse, admission to which was a disgrace and a last refuge, regarded with dread and hatred. The Poor Law has gone but its traditions remain. Slowly we have learned that any institution for the old encourages senility, while every effort to help them to live their own lives in a place of their own encourages independence and zest for life.

> Probably the first thing for anyone to learn who has old people to care for is the need to allow them the utmost freedom of action, to realise that their personality is still individual and that social significance is essential to happiness. It is all too easy to take the attitude that the old are past doing anything and encourage resting and doing nothing. This is a mistaken kindness, though it may be an easy way of satisfying the

113

conscience compared with the more exacting way of continual encouragement to be active, to go out, to find worthwhile occupation. The
latter course, however, is much more likely to promote happiness and to
forestall the troubles which may arise later on, from infirmity and
apathy.[14]

The de-institutionalisation of the treatment of mental illness began in
the eighteenth century when William Tuke founded the York Retreat,
and when Pinel in the same year (1792) struck off the chains from his
mad patients at Bicêtre. But in the nineteenth century, with what
Kathleen Jones calls 'the triumph of legalism', the pattern was laid down
of huge isolated lunatic asylums as a sinister appendage to the Poor Law,
– the heritage against which the modern pioneers have to struggle.
Kropotkin, in his remarkable lecture on prisons, delivered in Paris in
1887, took Pinel as the starting point for the 'community care' which is
now declared policy for mental health:

It will be said, however, there will always remain some people, the sick,
if you wish to call them that, who constitute a danger to society. Will it
not be necessary somehow to rid ourselves of them, or at least prevent
them from harming others?

No society, no matter how little intelligent, will need such an absurd
solution, and this is why. Formerly the insane were looked upon as
possessed by demons and were treated accordingly. They were kept in
chains in places like stables, riveted to the walls like wild beasts. But
along came Pinel, a man of the Great Revolution, who dared to remove
their chains and tried treating them as brothers. 'You will be devoured
by them,' cried the keepers. But Pinel dared. Those who were believed
to be wild beasts gathered around Pinel and proved by their attitude that
he was right in believing in the better side of human nature even when
the intelligence is clouded by disease. Then the cause was won. They
stopped chaining the insane.

Then the peasants of the little Belgian village, Gheel, found something better. They said: 'Send us your insane. We will give them
absolute freedom.' They adopted them into their families, they gave
them places at their tables, the chance alongside them to cultivate their
fields and a place among their young people at their country balls. 'Eat,
drink, and dance with us. Work, run about the fields and be free.' That
was the system, that was all the science the Belgian peasant had. And
liberty worked a miracle. The insane became cured. Even those who
had incurable, organic lesions became sweet, tractable members of the
family like the rest. The diseased mind would always work in an
abnormal fashion but the heart was in the right place. They cried it was a
miracle. The cures were attributed to a saint and a virgin. But this virgin

was liberty and the saint was work in the fields and fraternal treatment.

At one of the extremes of the immense 'space between mental disease and crime' of which Maudsley speaks, liberty and fraternal treatment have worked their miracle. They will do the same at the other extreme.[15]

Very slowly public sentiment and official policy have been catching up with this attitude. 'The first reform in the care of the mentally ill in America put the insane into state hospitals', writes J. B. Martin, 'the second reform is now in progress – to get them out again.'[16] Exactly the same is true of Britain. Evidence has been piling up for years to indicate that the institution manufactures madness. One key piece of research (by Hilliard and Munday at the Fountain Mental Deficiency Hospital) indicated that 54 per cent of the 'high-grade' patients were not in fact intellectually defective. Commenting in the light of this on 'the false impression of the problem of mental deficiency' resulting from present classifications, they remarked that 'such patients may be socially incompetent, but in many cases institutional life itself has aggravated their emotional difficulties.'[17]

The law itself has changed, sweeping away the whole process of certification and seeking the treatment of mental sickness like any other illness and mental deficiency like any physical handicap. Outpatient facilities, occupation centres and the variety of provisions known as 'community care' are intended to replace institutions wherever possible. And yet every year still brings a fresh crop of stories of grotesque conditions in allegedly therapeutic institutions, of terrible ill-treatment of helpless patients, or of the continued illegal detention of people who, years ago, had been placed in an institution because they were a nuisance to their relations or to a local authority and who had, over the years, been reduced to a state of premature senility by the institution itself.

But why, in the face of known facts about the harmful effects of institutions, and in the face of the officially declared policy of 'community care', have we failed, in spite of some glowing exceptions, to de-institutionalise mental illness? The answer is not merely the parsimony of public spending on mental health, it has two other important components. How can we adopt a policy of 'the replacement of a custodial authoritarian system by a permissive and tolerant culture in which the patients are encouraged to be themselves and share their feelings,'[18] when the staff themselves are organised in the rigid and authoritarian hierarchy that characterises every hospital? The people whose lives are spent in closest contact with the patients are themselves at the bottom of the pyramid of bullying and exploitation: there is no 'permissive and tolerant culture' for them, let alone for the inmates (This aspect of institutions is brilliantly illuminated in Erving Goffman's book *Asylums.*) The other factor is what the PEP report on community mental health calls the 'important irrational component' in public attitudes to deviancy. [19] Dr Joshua Bierer remarked that 'I and my colleagues are convinced that it is our own anxiety which forces us to lock people up, to brand them and make them criminals. I believe if we can overcome our own anxiety and treat adults and adolescents as members of the community, we will create fewer mental patients and fewer criminals.'[20]

There are indeed some people whose presence in ordinary society arouses such anxiety or hostility or fear, or for whose welfare it is so unwilling to assume responsibility in its normal primary groups like the family, that the special institutions we have discussed were established to contain them: asylums for the insane, orphanages for homeless children, the workhouse for the poor and aged, barracks for the defenders of the state, prisons and reformatories for those who transgress and get caught. Discipline, routine, obedience and submission were the characteristics sought in the well-regulated institution, best obtained in an enclosed environment, away from the distractions, comforts, seductions and dangerous liberties of ordinary society. In the nineteenth century – the great institution-building age – indeed, the same characteristics were sought in the ordinary 'open' institutions of outside society, the factory, the school, the developing civil service, the patriarchal family.

The prison is simply the ultimate institution, and every effort to reform the institution leaves its fundamental character untouched. It is, as Merfyn Turner says, 'an embarrassment to those who support the system it personifies, and a source of despair for those who would change it'. Godwin underlined the basic dilemma as long ago as the 1790s:

> The most common method pursued in depriving the offender of the liberty he has abused is to erect a public jail, in which offenders of every description are thrust together, and left to form among themselves what species of society they can. Various circumstances contribute to imbue them with habits of indolence and vice, and to discourage industry; and no effort is made to remove or soften these circumstances. It cannot be necessary to expatiate upon the atrociousness of this system. Jails are, to a proverb, seminaries of vice; and he must be an uncommon proficient in the passion and the practice of injustice, or a man of sublime virtue, who does not come out of them a much worse man than when he entered.[21]

And in the 1880s, Kropotkin (who originated the definition of prisons as 'universities of crime') explained the futility of attempts at reform:

> Whatever changes are introduced in the prison regime, the problem of second offenders does not decrease. That is inevitable: it must be so – the prison kills all the qualities in a man which make him best

adapted to community life. It makes him the kind of person who will inevitably return to prison ...
I might propose that a Pestalozzi be placed at the head of each prison ... I might also propose that in the place of the present guards, ex-soldiers and ex-policemen, sixty Pestalozzis be substituted. But, you will ask, where are we to find them? A pertinent question. The great Swiss teacher would certainly refuse to be a prison guard, for, basically, the principle of all prisons is wrong because it deprives men of liberty. So long as you deprive a man of his liberty, you will not make him better. You will cultivate habitual criminals.[22]

One of the things that emerges from the study of institutions is the existence of a recognisable dehumanised institutional character. In its ultimate form it was described by the psychiatrist Bruno Bettelheim in his book *The Informed Heart* (where he relates his previous studies of concentration camp behaviour and of emotionally disturbed children to the human condition in modern mass society). Bettelheim was a prisoner at Dachau and Buchenwald, and he describes those prisoners who were known as *Muselmänner* ('moslems'), the walking corpses who 'were so deprived of affect, self-esteem, and every form of stimulation, so totally exhausted, both physically and emotionally, that they had given the environment total power over them. They did this when they gave up trying to exercise any further influence over their life and environment'.[23] His terrible description of the ultimate institutional man goes on:

> But even the moslems, being organisms, could not help reacting somehow to their environment, and this they did by depriving it of the power to influence them as subjects in any way whatsoever. To achieve this, they had to give up responding to it all, and became objects, but with this they gave up being persons. At this point such men still obeyed orders, but only blindly or automatically; no longer selectively or with inner reservation or any hatred at being so abused. They still looked about, or at least moved their eyes around. The looking stopped much later, though even then they still moved their bodies when ordered, but never did anything on their own any more. Typically, this stopping of action began when they no longer lifted their legs as they walked, but only shuffled them. When finally even the looking about on their own stopped, they soon died.[24]

This description has a recognisable affinity to the behaviour observed in 'normal' institutions. 'Often the children sit inert or rock themselves for hours,' says Dr Bowlby of institution children. 'Go and watch them staring at the radiator, waiting to die,' says Brian Abel-Smith of institutional pensioners. Dr Russell Barton gave this man-made disease the

The Breakdown of Welfare

name *institutional neurosis* and described its clinical features in mental hospitals, its differential diagnosis, aetiology, treatment and prevention. It is, he says,

> a disease characterised by apathy, lack of initiative, loss of interest, especially in things of an impersonal nature, submissiveness, apparent inability to make plans for the future, lack of individuality, and sometimes a characteristic posture and gait. Permutations of these words and phrases, 'institutionalised', 'dull', 'apathetic', 'withdrawn', 'inaccessible', 'solitary', 'unoccupied', 'lacking in initiative', 'lacking in spontaneity', 'uncommunicative', 'simple', 'childish', 'gives no trouble', 'has settled down well', 'is cooperative', should always make one suspect that the process of institutionalisation has produced neurosis.[25]

He associates seven factors with the environment in which the disease occurs in mental hospitals: (1) Loss of contact with the outside world. (2) Enforced idleness. (3) Bossiness of medical and nursing staff. (4) Loss of personal friends, possessions, and personal events. (5) Drugs. (6) Ward atmosphere. (7) Loss of prospects outside the institution. Other writers have called the condition 'psychological institutionalism' or 'prison stupor', and many years ago Lord Brockway, in his book on prisons, depicted the type exactly in his description of the Ideal Prisoner: 'The man who has no personality: who is content to become a mere cog in the prison machine; whose mind is so dull that he does not feel the hardship of separate confinement; who has nothing to say to his fellows; who has no desires, except to feed and sleep, who shirks responsibility for his own existence and consequently is quite ready to live at others' orders, performing the allotted task, marching here and there as commanded, shutting the door of his cell upon his own confinement as required.'[26]

This is the ideal type of Institution Man, the kind of person who fits the system of public institutions which we have inherited from the past. It is no accident that it is also the ideal type for the bottom people of all authoritarian institutions. It is the ideal soldier (theirs not to reason why), the ideal worshipper (Have thine own way, Lord/Have thine own way/Thou art the potter/I am the clay), the ideal worker (You're not paid to think, just get on with it), the ideal wife (a chattel), the ideal child (seen but not heard) – the ideal product of the Education Act of 1870.

The institutions were a microcosm, or in some cases a caricature, of the society that produced them. Rigid, authoritarian, hierarchical, the virtues they sought were obedience and subservience. But the people who sought to break down the institutions, the pioneers of the changes which are slowly taking place, or which have still to be fought for, were motivated by different values. The key words in *their* vocabulary have been love, sympathy, permissiveness, and instead of institutions they have postulated families, communities, leaderless groups, autonomous groups. The qualities they have sought to foster are self-reliance, autonomy, self-respect, and, *as a consequence*, social responsibility, mutual respect and mutual aid.

When we compare the Victorian antecedents of our public institutions with the organs of working-class mutual aid in the same period the very names speak volumes. On the one side the Workhouse, the Poor Law Infirmary, the National Society for the Education of the Poor in Accordance with the Principles of the Established Church; and, on the other, the *Friendly* Society, the Sick *Club*, the *Cooperative* Society, the Trade *Union*. One represents the tradition of fraternal and autonomous associations springing up from below, the other that of authoritarian institutions directed from above.

It is important to note that the servants of the institution are as much its victims as the inmates. Russell Barton says that 'it is my impression that an authoritarian attitude is the rule rather than the exception' in mental hospitals, and he relates this to the fact that the nurse herself is 'subject to a process of institutionalisation in the nurses' home where she lives'. He finds it useless to blame any individual, for 'individuals change frequently but mental hospitals have remained unchanged', and he suggests that the fault lies with the administrative structure. Richard Titmuss, in his study of 'The Hospital and its Patients' attributes the barrier of silence so frequently met with in ordinary hospitals to 'the effect on people of working and living in a closed institution with rigid social hierarchies and codes of behaviour ... These people tend to deal with their insecurity by attempting to limit responsibility, and increase efficiency through the formulation of rigid rules and regulations and by developing an authoritative and protective discipline. The barrier of silence is one device employed to maintain authority. We find it used in many different settings when we look at other institutions where the relationship between the staff and the inmates is not a happy one.'[27]

And John Vaizey, remarking that 'everything in our social life is capable of being institutionalised, and it seems to me that our political energies should be devoted to restraining institutions' says that 'above all ... institutions give inadequate people what they want – power. Army officers, hospital sisters, prison warders - many of these people are inadequate and unfulfilled and they lust for power and control.'[28] In *The Criminal and His Victim*, von Hentig takes this view further: 'The police force and the ranks of prison officers attract many aberrant characters because they afford legal channels for pain-inflicting, power-wielding behaviour, and because these very positions confer upon their holders a large degree of immunity, this in turn causes psychopathic dispositions to grow more and more disorganised ...'[29] The point is emphasised with many telling illustrations in a modern anarchist classic, Alex Comfort's *Authority and Delinquency in the Modern State*.

The anarchist approach is clear: the breakdown of institutions into small units in the wider society, based on self-help and mutual support, like Synanon or Alcoholics Anonymous, or the many other supportive groups of this kind which have sprung up outside the official machinery of social welfare. Brian Abel-Smith (by no means an anarchist), when asked how we should rebuild and restructure the social services so that they really serve, replied:

> We would rebuild hospitals on modern lines – outpatients' departments or health centres, with a few beds tucked away in the corners. We would close the mental deficiency colonies and build new villas with small wards. How many could be looked after by quasi-housemothers in units of eight just like good local authorities are doing for children deprived of a normal home life? How many could be looked after at home if there were proper occupational centres and domiciliary services? We would plough up the sinister old mental hospitals and build small ones in or near the towns. We would pull down most of the institutions for old people and provide them with suitable housing . . . We would provide a full range of occupations at home and elsewhere for the disabled, the aged and the sick.[30]

And an anarchist approach to the penal institution? There is none, except to shut it down. The organisation called Radical Alternatives to Prison has listed twelve existing alternatives within the community, each of which is likely to be more effective than incarceration by impersonal, punitive and incompetent authorities, in enabling 'offenders' of different kinds to play a part as creative and influential members of society.[31]

Within the structure of social security as at present constituted, social welfare as a substitute for social justice – the most anarchical feature is the rapid growth of Claimants' Unions. This is a direct reaction to the way in which a so-called social insurance scheme has been institutionalised into a punitive, inquisitorial bureaucracy which declines to reveal to the 'clients' the basis on which payments are made or withheld.[32] Anna Coote's account of the Claimants' Unions notes that: 'Their growth has been entirely spontaneous, like the recent mushrooming of tenants' associations, play groups, neighbourhood newspapers and advice centres. They have no political affiliations and each one is anxious to maintain its independence, not to be controlled or influenced by any organisation. All Claimants' Unions are formed at grass-roots level amongst the claimants themselves – and in response to a specific need.'[33]

She makes the very significant observation that members of a Claimants' Union treat the social security office like home. 'They stand around exchanging information, conferring in corners, organising, handing out leaflets and words of encouragement' while 'claimants who don't belong to a union tend to sit still, without talking, looking anxious'.

A multiplicity of mutual aid organisations among claimants, patients, victims, represents the most potent lever for change in transforming the welfare state into a genuine welfare society, in turning community care into a caring community.

Chapter XIII

HOW DEVIANT DARE YOU GET?

In a free society you would have to come to terms with yourself and with others like yourself, with the man who backs his car into yours, with the man next door who has to feed three times as many mouths as you do, with the drunks who get into your garden. You would have to sort things out with them yourself, instead of having social workers or political parties or policemen or shop stewards to do the job for you, and in the process you would be forced to face up to what sort of person you yourself really were.

PETER BROWN, *Smallcreep's Day*

Every anarchist propagandist would agree that the aspect of anarchist ideas of social organisation which people find hardest to swallow is the anarchist rejection of the law, the legal system and the agencies of law-enforcement. They may ruefully agree with our criticism of the methods of the police, the fallibility of the courts, lawyers and judges, the barbarity of the penal system and the fatuity of the legislature. But they remain sceptical about the idea of a society in which the protection offered by the law is absent, and unconvinced that there are alternatives more desirable than 'the rule of law' which, with all its admitted failings, imperfections and abuses, is regarded as a precious achievement of civilised society and the best guarantee of the liberty of the individual citizen.

Maybe we are not worried by the mingled incredulity and bewilderment which meets our bland declaration that society should do away with the police and the law; perhaps we are perfectly satisfied to contemplate our own feeling that we can do without them; or perhaps we just enjoy a sense of revolutionary rectitude and superiority by deriding them. But it is our fellow-citizens that we have to convince if we are really concerned with gaining acceptance for the anarchist point of view.

The characteristic anarchist answer to the question of how an anarchist society would cope with criminal acts runs something like this: (a)
most crimes are of theft in one form or another, and in a society in
which real property and productive property were communally held and
personal property shared out on a more equitable basis, the incentive for
theft would disappear; (b) crimes of violence not originating in theft
would dwindle away since a genuinely permissive and non-competitive
society would not produce personalities prone to violence; (c) motoring
offences would not present the problems that they do now because
people would be more socially conscious and responsible, would tend to
use public transport when the private car had lost its status, and in a
more leisured society would lose the pathological love of speed and
aggressiveness that you see on the roads today; (d) in a decentralised
society vast urban conglomerations would cease to exist and people
would be more considerate and concerned for their neighbours. But the
difficulty about this kind of argument is that it brings the obvious
response that it calls for a new kind of human being, a social paragon of a
kind we do not often meet in real life. No, replies the anarchist, it calls
for a different kind of human environment, the kind that we are seeking
to build. But the trouble is, as an American criminologist, Paul Tappan,
put it, that as a society we *prefer* the social problems that surround us 'to
the consequences of deliberate and heroic efforts so drastically to change
the culture that man could live in uncomplicated adjustment to an
uncomplicated world'.

Any standard definition of the concepts of law, crime and law-enforcement will indicate that they are incompatible with the idea of anarchy:

> *Law:* The expressed will of the state. A command or a prohibition
> emanating from the authorised agencies of the state, and backed up by
> the authority and the capacity to exercise force which is characteristic of
> the state ...
>
> *Crime:* A violation of the criminal law, i.e. a breach of the conduct code
> specifically sanctioned by the state, which through its legislative agencies
> defines crimes and their penalties, and through its administrative
> agencies prosecutes offenders and imposes and administers punishments.
>
> *Police:* Agents of the law charged with the responsibility of maintaining
> law and order among the citizens.[1]

It is possible, of course, to re-define the concept of law in a non-legal-
istic sense: in the sense of common law, the embodiment of pre-existing
social custom, or in a looser sociological sense as the whole body of rules
of all sorts that exist in a society; and it is possible to re-define the
concept of crimes as anti-social acts – whether or not they are illegal
acts. The nineteenth-century criminologist, Garofallo, enlarged the
definition of crime to 'any action which goes against the prevalent

norms of probity and compassion', and his modern successor E. H.
Sutherland, in his study of white-collar crime, insisted that 'legal classification should not confine the work of the criminologist and he should
be completely free to push across the barriers of definition when he sees
non-criminal behaviour which resembles criminal behaviour'. (Alex
Comfort has done this brilliantly from the anarchist standpoint in his
castigation of lawmakers and power-seekers in *Authority and Deliquency
in the Modern State.*)

On the other hand it is scarcely possible for us to re-define the police,
the agents of law-enforcement, in a way that is shorn of authoritarian
connotations. Obviously in our society the police fulfil certain *social*
functions, but everyone will agree that their primary purpose is to fulfil
governmental functions. John Coatman's volume *The Police* in the Home
University Library, for instance, declares that our police system is 'the
pith and marrow of the English conduct of government' and that the
policeman themselves are the 'guardians of the established system of
government'. With which we would all agree.

No, there is no non-authoritarian equivalent for the policeman,
except for the concept which we would now call 'social control', of the
means by which individuals and communities may protect themselves
from anti-social acts. This concept first appeared in anarchist thought in
Godwin's *Political Justice* where, adopting the decentralist approach to the
question, he declared: 'If communities . . . were contented with a small
district, with a proviso of confederation in cases of necessity, every individual would then live in the public eye; and the disapprobation of his
neighbours, a species of coercion, not derived from the caprice of men
but from the system of the universe, would inevitably oblige him either
to reform or to emigrate.'[2] Many people, I fear, especially those who
have experience of living under the censorious eyes of neighbours in a
village, would find this a rather unattractive way of inhibiting anti-social
behaviour, and because it also inhibits many other varieties of non-
conforming behaviour as well, would prefer the anonymous city life.

This insistence on a more closely-knit community as the means by
which society can 'contain' anti-social acts recurs time and again in the
writings of Kropotkin, who of all the classical anarchist thinkers devoted
most consideration to the question of crime, the law and the penal
system:

> Of course in every society, no matter how well organised, people will
> be found with easily aroused passions, who may, from time to time,
> commit anti-social deeds. But what is necessary to prevent this is to give
> their passions a healthy direction, another outlet.
>
> Today we live too isolated. Private property has led us to an egotistic
> individualism in all our mutual relations. We know one another only

slightly; our po̱ ̱s of contact are too rare. But we have seen in history examples of a communal life which is more intimately bound together – the 'composite family' in China, the agrarian communes, for example. There people really know one another. By force of circumstances they must aid one another materially and morally.

Family life, based on the original community, has disappeared. A new family, based on community of aspirations, will take its place. In this family people will be obliged to know one another, to aid one another and to lean on one another for moral support on every occasion. And this mutual prop will prevent the great number of anti-social acts which we see today.[3]

The concept was first given the name *social control* by Edward Allsworth Ross in a book of that name published in 1901, in which he cited instances of 'frontier' societies where, through unorganised or informal measures, order is effectively maintained without benefit of legally constituted authority: 'Sympathy, sociability, the sense of justice and resentment are competent, under favourable circumstances', wrote Ross, 'to work out by themselves a true, natural order, that is to say, an order without design or art.' Today the term social control has been extended to refer to 'the aggregate of values and norms by means of which tensions and conflicts between individuals and groups are resolved or mitigated in order to maintain the solidarity of some more inclusive group, and also to the arrangements through which these values and norms are communicated and instilled . . . Social control as the regulation of behaviour by values and norms is to be contrasted with regulation by force. These two modes are not, of course, entirely separable in actual social life . . . But the distinction is valuable and important.'[4]

George C. Homans in *The Human Group* puts the distinction thus: 'The process by which conformity is achieved we call *social control* if we are thinking of compliance with norms, or *authority* if we are thinking of obedience to orders.' It is the size and scale of the community which, in the opinion of the sociologists, diminishes the effectiveness of social control: 'It is only as groups grow large, and come to be composed of individuals with conflicting moral standards, that informal controls yield priority to those that are formal, such as laws and codes.'[5]

One of the few observers of modern city life to think about the way social control actually operates in the contemporary urban environment is Jane Jacobs, who discusses the function of streets and their pavements or sidewalks in these terms:

> To keep the city safe is a fundamental task of a city's streets and its side-walks ... Great cities ... differ from towns and suburbs in basic ways, and one of these is that cities are, by definition, full of strangers ...

The bedrock attitude of a successful city district is that a person must feel personally safe and secure on the street among all those strangers. He must not feel automatically menaced by them ... The first thing to understand is that the public peace – the sidewalk and street peace – of cities is not kept primarily by the police, necessary as the police are. It is kept primarily by an intricate, almost unconscious, network of voluntary controls and standards among the people themselves, and enforced by the people themselves. In some city areas – older public housing projects and streets with a very high population turnover are often conspicuous examples – the keeping of public sidewalk law and order is left almost entirely to the police and special guards. Such places are jungles. No amount of police can enforce civilisation where the normal, casual enforcement of it has broken down.'[6]

Her point is that the populous street has an unconscious do-it-yourself surveillance system of *eyes* in the street, the eyes of the residents and the users of shops, cafes, news-stands and so on:

Safety on the streets by surveillance and mutual policing of one another sounds grim, but in real life it is not grim. The safety of the streets works best, most casually, and with least frequent taint of suspicion or hostility precisely where people are using and most enjoying the city streets voluntarily and are least conscious, normally, that they are policing . . .

In settlements that are smaller and simpler than big cities, controls on acceptable public behaviour, if not on crime, seem to operate with greater or lesser success through a web of reputation, gossip, approval, disapproval and sanctions, all of which are powerful if people know each other and words travel. But a city's streets, which must control not only the behaviour of the people of the city but also of visitors from suburbs and towns who want to have a big time away from the gossip and sanctions at home, have to operate by more direct, straightforward methods. It is a wonder cities have solved such an inherently difficult problem at all. And yet in many streets they do it magnificently.[7]

The English reader of Mrs Jacobs' book will by now no longer be amazed by her assumption of the insecurity of the American citizen in public places from 'rape, muggings, beatings, hold-ups and the like'. Today, she declares, 'barbarism has taken over many city streets, or people fear it has, which comes to much the same thing in the end'. In spite of her faith in the effectiveness of informal social control, nothing is going to destroy *her* belief in the necessity of the police. The terrifying breakdown of social cohesion in the American city, in spite of intense institutionalised police surveillance equipped with every sophisticated aid to public control, illustrates that social behaviour depends upon mutual responsibility rather than upon the policeman. The most honest and unequivocal attempt to grasp this particular nettle from the anarchist point of view comes from Errico Malatesta:

> This necessary defence against those who violate, not the *status quo*, but the deepest feelings which distinguish man from the beasts, is one of the pretexts by which governments justify their existence. We must eliminate all the social causes of crime, we must develop in man brotherly feelings, and mutual respect; we must, as Fourier put it, seek useful alternatives to crime. But if, and so long as, there are criminals, either people will find the means, and have the energy, to defend themselves directly against them, or the police and the magistrature will reappear, and with them, government. We do not solve a problem by denying its existence ...
>
> We can, with justification, fear that this necessary defence against crime could be the beginning of, and the pretext for, a new system of oppression and privilege. It is the mission of the anarchists to see that this does not happen. By seeking the causes of each crime and making every effort to eliminate them; by making it impossible for anyone to derive personal advantage out of the detection of crime, and by leaving it to the interested groups themselves to take whatever steps they deem necessary for their defence; by accustoming ourselves to consider criminals as brothers who have strayed, as sick people needing loving treatment, as one would for any victim of hydrophobia or dangerous lunatic – it will be possible to reconcile the complete freedom of all with defence against those who obviously and dangerously threaten it ...
>
> For us the carrying out of social duties must be a voluntary act, and we only have the right to intervene with material force against those who offend against others *violently* and prevent them from living in peace. Force, physical restraint, must only be used against attacks of violence and for no other reason than that of self-defence. But who will judge? Who will provide the necessary defence? Who will establish what measures of restraint are to be used? We do not see any other way than that of leaving it to the interested parties, to the people, that is the mass of citizens, who will act differently according to the circumstances and according to their different degrees of social development. We must, above all, avoid the creation of bodies specialising in police work; perhaps something will be lost in repressive efficiency but we will avoid the creation of the instrument of every tyranny. In every respect the injustice, and transitory violence of the people is better than the leaden rule, the legalised state violence of the judiciary and police. We are, in any case, only one of the forces acting in society, and history will advance, as always, in the direction of the resultant of all the forces.[8]

Three things stand out from Malatesta's observations. Firstly, he recognised that any and every do-it-yourself justice system would have a tendency to harden into an institution. The difficulty is that this might very well be for very good reasons: the attempt to give the accused a 'fair' trial (for I take it that the restraint of offenders would include some procedure to find out whether the accused committed the offence). If the offender is to be more fairly treated than he would be under existing systems of jurisprudence, certain safeguards which exist in the present system must survive in any *ad hoc* arrangement. There must be recognition of the principle of *habeas corpus*, the accused must be told what he is accused of, he must be given facilities to defend himself, there must be generally accepted rules of evidence, and so on. The history of revolutionary regimes is littered with committees of public safety, people's courts and similar 'revolutionary' bodies, which have turned out to be just as dubious a proposition, from the point of view of those who are brought before them, as the bourgeois institutions they replaced. The more fortunate of the East European countries have slowly reintroduced 'Western' juridical principles and safeguards – to everybody's relief. The problem in Malatesta's terms is how to build these principles of 'natural justice' into popular bodies which nevertheless retain an impermanent non-institutional character.

The second thing that stands out in the passage from Malatesta is his faith in 'the people'; a point which adversaries would gleefully take up, drawing attention to the fact that he is presupposing a different kind of people. We know that our 'people' are as vindictive as our judges. Three-quarters of the population of Britain are said to favour the re-introduction of capital punishment, and an even larger proportion the re-introduction of flogging and birching. Here we are at the crux of the difficulty which we anarchists have in getting our ideas on this subject taken seriously. There seems to be an immense anxiety and fear floating around in our society which is out of proportion to actual dangers. People are afraid of defencelessness. (In another field this explains why people cannot accept the idea of disarmament – they believe that they are actually being defended.) Observation of the general intense preoccupation and fascination with crime certainly seems to bear out the psychoanalytical theory that society not only makes its criminals, but that it *needs* them, and consequently seduces its deviant individuals into the 'acting-out' of criminal roles.

'Society', wrote Paul Reiwald, 'opposed the innovators with determined resistance . . . Society did not wish to abandon the principle of an eye for an eye; it did not wish to be deprived of its long observed relations to the criminal and it did not wish to have the "contrary ones" taken from it.'[9] Ruth Eissler expresses it even more dramatically: 'Society, by using its criminals as scapegoats and by trying to destroy them because it is unable to bear the reflection of its own guilt, actually stabs at its own heart.'[10]

128

Obviously some people are conspicuously lacking in this pent-up anxiety and guilt, the kind of people who are singularly successful in supportive, rather than punitive, work with delinquents or deviants, people who are sufficiently at ease with themselves to cope with the mental strain, the irritation and time-consuming tedium which our deviants frequently impose on us. If we want to change society it is probably more important for us to find out what produces people like *them* than to find out what makes delinquents. This is important for the whole idea of the social control of anti-social behaviour. What is anti-social? If this question is to be decided by a bunch of censorious busybodies we can well imagine people saying 'No thanks. I'd rather have The Law.' There must be room for deviance in society, and there must be support for the right to deviate. This, I suppose, is the basis of Durkheim's celebrated observation that crime itself is a social norm, 'a factor in public health, an integral part of all healthy societies' since a crimeless society would be an ossified society with an unimaginable degree of social conformity, and that 'crime implies not only that the way remains open to necessary changes but that in certain cases it precipitates these changes'. As anarchists – criminals ourselves in some people's view – we should be the first to appreciate this.

And this brings us to Malatesta's final point, his observation that 'we are, in any case, only one of the forces acting in society'. It is not a matter of a hypothetical anarchist society, but of any society, now or in the future, where different social philosophies and attitudes coexist and conflict. There will always be anti-social acts, and there will always be people with an urge to punish, to maintain a whole punitive machinery with everything that it entails. If we do not discover and make use of methods of *containing* such acts within society or of evolving a form of society capable of containing them, we shall certainly continue to be the victims of those authoritarian solutions which others are so ready and eager to apply.

Chapter XIV

ANARCHY AND A PLAUSIBLE FUTURE

For the earlier part of my life I was quieted by being told that ours was the richest country in the world, until I woke up to know that what I meant by riches was learning and beauty, and music and art, coffee and omelettes; perhaps in the coming days of poverty we may get more of these ...

W. R. LETHABY, *Form in Civilisation*

This book has illustrated the arguments for anarchism, not from theories, but from actual examples of tendencies which already exist, alongside much more powerful and dominant authoritarian methods of social organisation. The important question is, therefore, not whether anarchy is possible or not, but whether we can so enlarge the scope and influence of libertarian methods that they become the normal way in which human beings organise their society. Is an anarchist society possible?

We can only say, from the evidence of human history, that no kind of society is impossible. If you are powerful enough and ruthless enough you can impose almost any kind of social organisation on people – for a while. But you can only do so by methods which, however natural and appropriate they may be for any other kind of 'ism' – acting on the well-known principle that you can't make an omelette without breaking eggs, are repugnant to anarchists, unless they see themselves as yet another of those revolutionary elites 'leading the people' to the promised land. You can impose authority but you cannot impose freedom. An anarchist society is improbable, not because anarchy is unfeasible, or unfashionable, or unpopular, but because human society is not like that, because, as Malatesta put it in the passage quoted in the last chapter, 'we are, in any case, only one of the forces acting in society'.

The degree of social cohesion implied in the idea of 'an anarchist society' could only occur in a society so embedded in the cake of custom that the idea of *choice* among alternative patterns of social behaviour simply did not occur to people. I cannot imagine that degree of unanimity and I would dislike it if I could, because the idea of choice is crucial to any philosophy of freedom and spontaneity. So we don't have to worry about the boredom of utopia: we shan't get there. But what results from this conclusion? One response would be to stress anarchism as an ideal of personal liberation, ceasing to think of changing society, except by example. Another would be to conclude that because no roads lead to utopia no road leads anywhere, an attitude which, in the end, is identical with the utopian one because it asserts that there are no partial, piecemeal, compromise or temporary solutions, only *one* attainable or unattainable final solution. But, as Alexander Herzen put it over a century ago: 'A goal which is infinitely remote is not a goal at all, it is a deception. A goal must be closer – at the very least the labourer's wage or pleasure in the work performed. Each epoch, each generation, each life has had, and has, its own experience, and the end of each generation must be itself.'[1]

The choice between libertarian and authoritarian solutions is not a once-and-for-all cataclysmic struggle, it is a series of running engagements, most of them never concluded, which occur, and have occurred, throughout history. Every human society, except the most totalitarian of utopias or anti-utopias, is a plural society with large areas which are not in conformity with the officially imposed or declared values. An example of this can be seen in the alleged division of the world into capitalist and communist blocks: there are vast areas of capitalist societies which are not governed by capitalist principles, and there are many aspects of the socialist societies which cannot be described as socialist. You might even say that the only thing that makes life liveable in the capitalist world is the unacknowledged non-capitalist element within it, and the only thing that makes survival possible in the communist world is the unacknowledged capitalist element in it. This is why a controlled market is a left-wing demand in a capitalist economy – along with state control, while a free market is a left-wing demand in a communist society – along with workers' control. In both cases, the demands are for whittling away power from the centre, whether it is the power of the state or capitalism, or state-capitalism.

So what are the prospects for increasing the anarchist content of the real world? From one point of view the outlook is bleak: centralised power, whether that of government or super-government, or of private capitalism or the super-capitalism of giant international corporations, has never been greater. The prophesies of nineteenth-century anarchists like Proudhon and Bakunin about the power of the state over the citizen have a relevance today which must have seemed unlikely for their contemporaries.

From another standpoint the outlook is infinitely promising. The very growth of the state and its bureaucracy, the giant corporation and its privileged hierarchy, are exposing their vulnerability to non-cooperation, to sabotage, and to the exploitation of *their* weaknesses by the weak. They are also giving rise to parallel organisations, counter organisations, alternative organisations, which exemplify the anarchist method. Industrial mergers and rationalisation have bred the revival of the demand for workers' control, first as a slogan or a tactic like the work-in, ultimately as a destination. The development of the school and the university as broiler-houses for a place in the occupational pecking-order have given rise to the de-schooling movement and the idea of the anti-university. The use of medicine and psychiatry as agents of conformity has led to the idea of the anti-hospital and the self-help therapeutic group. The failure of Western society to house its citizens has prompted the growth of squatter movements and tenants' co-operatives. The triumph of the supermarket in the United States has begun a mush-rooming of food cooperatives. The deliberate pauperisation of those who cannot work has led to the recovery of self-respect through Claimants' Unions.

Community organisations of every conceivable kind, community newspapers, movements for child welfare, communal households have resulted from the new consciousness that local as well as central governments exploit the poor and are unresponsive to those who are unable to exert effective pressure for themselves. The 'rationalisation' of local administration in Britain into 'larger and more effective units' is evoking a response in the demand for neighbourhood councils. A new self-confidence and assertion of their right to exist on their own terms has sprung up among the victims of particular kinds of discrimination – black liberation, women's liberation, homosexual liberation, prisoners' liberation, children's liberation: the list is almost endless and is certainly going to get longer as more and more people become more and more conscious that society is organised in ways which deny them a place in the sun. In the age of mass politics and mass conformity, this is a magnificent re-assertion of individual value and of human dignity.

None of these movements is yet a threat to the power structure, and this is scarcely surprising since hardly any of them existed before the late 1960s. None of them fits into the framework of conventional politics. In fact, they don't speak the same language as the political parties. They talk the language of anarchism and they insist on anarchist principles of organisation, which they have learned not from political theory but from their own experience. They organise in loosely associated groups which are *voluntary, functional, temporary* and *small*. They depend, not on membership cards, votes, a special leadership and a herd of inactive followers but on small, functional groups which ebb and flow, group and regroup, according to the task in hand. They are networks, not pyramids.

At the very time when the 'irresistible trends of modern society' seemed to be leading us to a mass society of enslaved consumers they are reminding us of the truth that the irresistible is simply that which is not resisted. But obviously a whole series of partial and incomplete victories, of concessions won from the holders of power, will not lead to an anarchist society. But it will widen the scope of free action and the potentiality for freedom in the society we have. But such compromises of anarchist notions would have to be made, such authoritarian bedfellows chosen, for a frontal attack on the power structure, that the anarchist answer to cries for revolutionary unity is likely to be 'Whose noose are you inviting me to put round my neck this time?'

But in thinking about a plausible future, another factor has entered into the general consciousness since the late 1960s. So many books, so many reports, so many conferences have been devoted to it, that it is only necessary for me to state a few general propositions about it. The first is that the world's resources are finite. The second is that the wealthy economies have been exploiting the unrenewable resources at a rate which the planet cannot sustain. The third is that these 'developed' economies are also exploiting the resources of the 'Third World' countries as cheap raw materials. This means, not only that the Third World countries can never hope to achieve the levels of consumption of the rich world, but that the rich countries themselves cannot continue to consume at the present accelerating rate. The public debate around these issues is not about the truth of the contentions, it is simply about the question: How Soon? How soon before the fossil fuels run out? How soon before the Third World rises in revolt against international exploitation? How soon will we be facing the consequences of the nonviability of future economic growth? I leave aside the related questions about pollution and about population. But all these questions profoundly affect all our futures and the predictions we make about social change, whether we mean the changes we desire or the ones which circumstances force upon us. They also cut completely across accepted political categories, as do the policies of the ecology lobby or the environmental pressure groups in both Britain and the United States.

The growth economists, the politicians of both right and left, who envisaged an ever-expanding cycle of consumption, with the philosophy characterised by Kenneth Burke as Borrow, Spend, Buy, Waste, Want,[2] have just not caught up with future realities. If anyone has it is that minority among the young in the affluent countries who have consciously rejected the mass consumption society – its values as well as its dearly-bought products – and adopted, not out of puritanism but out of a different set of priorities, an earlier consumer philosophy: Eat it up,

133

wear it out, make it do, or do without. The editor of *The Ecologist* summed up the argument thus: 'affluence for everybody is an impossible dream: the world simply does not contain sufficient resources, nor could it absorb the heat and other waste generated by the immense amount of energy required. Indeed, the most important thing to realise, when we plan our future, is that affluence is both a local and a temporary phenomenon. Unfortunately it is the principal, if not the only, goal our industrial society gives us.' His journal in its 'Blueprint for Survival' has the distinction of being among the few commentaries on the crisis of environment and resources to go beyond predicting the consequences of continued population growth and depletion of resources, to envisaging the kind of physical and economic structure of life which its authors regard as indispensable for a viable future, drawing up a timetable for change for the century 1975-2075, to establish in that time 'a network of self-sufficient, self-regulating communities.'[3] The authors cheerfully accept the charge that their programme is unsophisticated and oversimplified, the implication being that if the reader can formulate a better alternative, or a different time-scale, he should do so. The interesting thing is that they have re-invented an older vision of the future. Back in the 1890s three men, equally unqualified as shareholders in Utopia Limited, formulated their prescriptions for the physical setting of a future society. William Morris, designer and socialist, wrote *News from Nowhere;* Peter Kropotkin, geographer and anarchist, wrote *Fields, Factories and Workshops*; and Ebenezer Howard, inventor and parliamentary shorthand writer, wrote *Tomorrow: A Peaceful Path to Real Reform.* Each of these blueprints for survival was more influential than its original readers could have supposed, though less than its author would have hoped. Morris's vision was totally irrelevant for the twentieth century, but his picture of a post-industrial, decentralised, state-free Britain in the twenty-first century, certainly makes sense for the new ecologically-aware generation, while any American will recognise the force of his backward glance at the future of the United States: 'For these lands, and, I say, especially the northern parts of America, suffered so terribly from the full force of the last days of civilisation, and became such horrible places to live in, that one may say that for nearly a hundred years the people of the northern parts of America have been engaged in gradually making a dwelling-place out of a stinking dust-heap ...'[4]

Howard's legacy is of course the new towns: his immediate purpose was to mobilise voluntary initiative for the building of one demonstration model, confident that its advantages would set in motion a large-scale adoption of the idea of urban dispersal in 'social cities', or what the TCPA calls 'a many-centred nexus of urban communities'. Lewis Mumford notes that 'By now, our neotechnic and biotechnic facilities have at last caught up with Howard's and Kropotkin's intuitions.

Howard's plan for canalising the flow of population, diverting it from the existing centres to new centres; his plan for decentralising industry and setting up both city and industry within a rural matrix, the whole planned to a human scale, is technologically far more feasible today than it was ...[5]

Kropotkin's own vision of the future, with industry decentralised, and the competition for markets replaced by local production and consumption while people themselves alternate brain work and manual work, is being realised in a political climate he hardly foresaw, in China, but is equally in harmony with the programme of the 'Blueprint for Survival':

> The scattering of industries over the country – so as to bring the factory amidst the fields, to make agriculture derive all those profits which it always finds in being combined with industry and to produce a combination of industrial with agricultural work – is surely the next step to be taken ... This step is imposed by the necessity for each healthy man and woman to spend a part of their lives in manual work in the free air; and it will be rendered the more necessary when the great social movements, which have now become unavoidable, come to disturb the present international trade, and compel each nation to revert to her own resources for her own maintenance.'[6]

The authors of the 'Blueprint', having set out their analysis of the crisis of population, resources and environment, sketch out what they see as a necessary and desirable future for the human habitat. They argue for decentralisation on several grounds. Their first reason is that it would 'promote the social conditions in which public opinion and full public participation in decision-making become as far as possible the means whereby communities are ordered'. Their second reason is that, on ecological grounds, they foresee a return to diversified farming instead of prairie-type crop-growing or factory-type livestock rearing, with production for a local market and the return of domestic sewage to the land, in the setting of 'a decentralised society of small communities where industries are small enough to be responsive to each community's needs'. Thirdly, they think it significant that 'the decreasing autonomy of communities and local regions, and the increasing centralisation of decision-making and authority in the cumbersome bureaucracies of the state, have been accompanied by the rise of self-conscious individualism, an individualism that feels threatened unless it is harped upon'.

They see the accumulation of material goods as the accompaniment of this self-conscious individualism (what others would call 'privatisation') and believe that the rewards of significant relationships and mutual responsibilities in a small community will provide ample compensation for the decreasing emphasis on consumption which will be essential for the conservation of resources and the minimisation of pollution. Their

135

final reason is that 'to deploy a population in small towns and villages is to reduce to the minimum its impact on the environment. This is because the actual urban superstructure required per inhabitant goes up radically as the size of the town increases beyond a certain point.' Affirming that they are *not* proposing inward-looking, self-obsessed, or closed communities, but in fact want 'an efficient and sensitive communications network between all communities', they conclude with the splendid declaration: 'We emphasise that our goal should be to create *community* feeling and *global* awareness, rather than that dangerous and sterile compromise which is nationalism.'[7]

But will it ever happen? Will this humane and essentially anarchistic vision of a workable future simply join all the other anarchical utopias of the past? Years ago George Orwell remarked:

> If one considers the probabilities one is driven to the conclusion that anarchism implies a low standard of living. It need not imply a hungry or uncomfortable world, but it rules out the kind of air-conditioned, chromium-plated, gadget-ridden existence which is now considered desirable and enlightened. The processes involved in making, say, an aeroplane are so complex as to be only possible in a planned, centralised society, with all the repressive apparatus that that implies. Unless there is some unpredictable change in human nature, liberty and efficiency must pull in opposite directions.[8]

This, from Orwell's point of view (he was not a lover of luxury) is not in itself a criticism of anarchism, and he is certainly right in thinking that an anarchist society would never build Concorde or land men on the moon. But were either of these technological triumphs efficient in terms of the resources poured into them and the results for the ordinary inhabitant of this planet? Size and resources are to the technologist what power is to the politician: he can never have too much of them. A different kind of society, with different priorities, would evolve a different technology: its bases already exist[9] and in terms of the tasks to be performed it would be far more 'efficient' than either Western capitalism or Soviet state-capitalism. Not only technology but also economics would have to be redefined. As Kropotkin envisaged it: 'Political economy tends more and more to become a science devoted to the study of the needs of men and of the means of satisfying them with the least possible waste of energy, that is, a sort of physiology of society.'[10]

But it is not in the least likely that states and governments, in either the rich or the poor worlds will, of their own volition, embark on the drastic change of direction which a consideration of our probable future demands. Necessity may reduce the rate of resource-consumption but the powerful and privileged will hang on to their share – both within nations and between nations. Power and privilege have never been

known to abdicate. This is why anarchism is bound to be a call to revolution. But what kind of revolution? Nothing has been said in this book
about the two great irrelevancies of discussion about anarchism: the false
antitheses between violence and nonviolence and between revolution
and reform. The most violent institution in our society is the state and it
reacts violently to efforts to take away its power. 'As Malatesta used to
say, you try to do your thing and they intervene, and then *you* are to
blame for the fight that happens.'[11] Does this mean that the effort should
not be made? A distinction has to be made between the violence of the
oppressor and the resistance of the oppressed.

Similarly, there is a distinction not between revolution and reform but
on the one hand between the kind of revolution which installs a
different gang of rulers or the kind of reform which makes oppression
more palatable or more efficient, and on the other those social changes,
whether revolutionary or reformist, through which people enlarge their
autonomy and reduce their subjection to external authority.

Anarchism in all its guises is an assertion of human dignity and
responsibility. It is not a programme for political change but an act of
social self-determination.

SOURCES AND REFERENCES

Chapter I

1   Vaclav Cerny, 'The Socialistic Year 1848 and its Heritage', *The Critical Monthly*, Nos. 1 and 2 (Prague, 1948).

2   Michael Bakunin, 'Letter to the Internationalists of the Romagna' 28 January 1872.

3   Fabian Tract No 4, *What Socialism Is* (London, 1886).

4   Pierre-Joseph Proudhon, *The Political Capacity of the Working Class* (Paris, 1864).

5   Peter Kropotkin, *Modern Science and Anarchism* (London, 1912).

6   The same, French edition (Paris, 1913).

7   George Benello, 'Wasteland Culture', *Our Generation*, Vol. 5, No. 2, (Montreal, 1967).

8   Martin Buber, 'Society and the State', *World Review*, (London, 1951).

9   Fred J. Cook, *The Warfare State* (London, 1963).

10 MacIver and Page, *Society* (London, 1948).

11 Simone Weil, 'Reflections on War', *Left Review*, (London, 1938).

12 Randolph Bourne, *The State,* Resistance Press, (New York, 1945). (first published 1919).

13 Peter Kropotkin, *op. cit.*

14 Camillo Berneri, *Kropotkin, His Federalist Ideas* (London, 1943).

15 David Wieck, 'The Habit of Direct Action', *Anarchy* 13, (London, 1962), reprinted in Colin Ward (ed.), *A Decade of Anarchy*, (London, Freedom Press, 1987).

16 Paul Goodman, *Like a Conquered Province* (New York, 1967).

17 Vernon Richards (ed.), *Malatesta: His Life and Ideas* (London, Freedom Press, 1965).

18 Theodore Draper in *Encounter*, August 1968.

Chapter II

1   *Fifty Million Volunteers*, Report on the Role of Voluntary Organisations and Youth in the Environment (London, 1972).

2   Graham Whiteman, 'Festival Moment', *Anarchy* 116, October 1970.

3   John Comerford, *Health the Unknown: The Story of the Peckham Experiment* (London, 1947). See also Innes Pearse and Lucy Crocker, *The Peckham Experiment* (London, 1943); *Biologists in Search of Material* by G. Scott Williamson and I. H. Pearse (London, 1938).

4   Edward Allsworth Ross, *Social Control* (New York, 1901).

5   See Homer Lane, *Talks to Parents and Teachers* (London, 1928); W. David Wills, *Homer Lane: A Biography* (London, 1964); Howard Jones: *Reluctant Rebels* (London, 1963).

6 August Aichhorn, *Wayward Youth* (London, 1925).

7 *ibid.*

8 John Berger, 'Freedom and the Czechs' (*New Society*, 29 August 1968).

9 Harry Schwartz, *Prague's 200 Days* (London, 1969).

10 *ibid.*

11 *The Listener,* 5 September 1958.

12 Ladislav Mnacko, *The Seventh Night* (London, 1969).

13 Schwartz, *op. cit.*

14 Daniel Guérin, 'The Czechoslovak Working Class and the Resistance Movement' in *Czechoslovakia and Socialism* (London, 1969).

15 *Encounter,* January 1957.

16 Tape-recording in the BBC Sound Archives.

17 Robert Lyon in *Peace News*, 20 February 1959.

18 Alan Burgess in the *Radio Times,* 13 February 1959.

19 Appendix III of Philip Windsor and Adam Roberts, *Czechoslovakia 1968* (London, 1969).

20 George Orwell, *Homage to Catalonia* (London, 1938).

21 Andy Anderson, *Hungary 1956* (London, 1964).

22 In Noam Chomsky, *American Power and the New Mandarins* (London, 1969).

23 *ibid.* The best available accounts in English of the collectivisation of industry and agriculture in the Spanish revolution are in Vernon Richards, *Lessons of the Spanish Revolution* (London, Freedom Press, 2nd ed. 1983) and Burnett Bolloten, *The Grand Camouflage* (London, 1961).

Chapter III

1 RIBA, *The Architect and His Office* (London, 1962).

2 Walter Gropius, an address given at the RIBA, April 1956.

3 Wilhelm Reich, Work Democracy in Action, *Annals of the Orgone Institute*, Vol. 1, 1944.

4 *ibid.*

5 Peter Kropotkin, *Fields, Factories and Workshops Tomorrow,* edited by Colin Ward (London, Freedom Press, 1985).

6 Richard Boston in *Peace News*, 23 February 1962.

7 Simon Nicholson, 'The Theory of Loose Parts', *Bulletin of Environmental Education*, April, 1972.

Chapter IV

1 Raymond Pirth, *Human Types* (London, 1970).

2 Peter Kropotkin, *Law and Authority*, reprinted in Baldwin (ed.), *Kropotkin's Revolutionary Pamphlets* (New York, 1927, 1968).

3   John Middleton and David Tait (eds), *Tribes without Rulers: Studies in African Segmentary Systems* (London, 1958).

4   *ibid.*

5   *ibid.*

6   Ernest Gellner, 'How to Live in Anarchy', *The Listener*, 3 April 1958.

7   Middleton and Tait, *op.cit.*

8   Peter Kropotkin, *Anarchism: Its Philosophy and Ideal*, reprinted in Baldwin, op.cit.

9   W. Grey Walter, 'The Development and Significance of Cybernetics', *Anarchy* 25, March 1963.

10 John D. McEwan, 'Anarchism and the Cybernetics of Self-organising Systems, *Anarchy* 31, September 1963, reprinted in Colin Ward (ed.), *A Decade of Anarchy*, (London, Freedom Press, 1987).

11 Donald Schon, *Beyond the Stable State* (London, 1971).

12 Mary Douglas in *The Listener*, 1971

13 Peter Kropotkin, article on *Anarchism* written in 1905 for *Encyclopaedia Britannica,* 11th edition. (Reprinted in *Anarchism & Anarchist Communism,* London, Freedom Press, 1987).

Chapter V

1   George Woodcock, *Anarchism: A History of Libertarian Ideas and Movements* (Cleveland 1962; London 1963).

2   P.-J. Proudhon, *Du Principe Federatif* quoted in Stewart Edwards (ed.) *Selected Writings of Pierre-Joseph Proudhon* (London, 1970).

3   Herbert Luethy, 'Has Switzerland a Future?', *Encounter,* December 1962.

4   See Theodore Roszak, 'The Case for Listener-supported Radio', *Anarchy* 93, November 1968.

5   'The Spies for Peace Story', *Anarchy* 29, July 1963.

Chapter VI

1   Philip Mairet, *Patrick Geddes* (London, 1959).

2   Town and Country Planning Act 1968, and *People and Planning: Report of the Committee on Public Participation in Planning* (Skeffington Report), (London: 1969).

3   Rayner Banham, Peter Hall, Paul Barker and Cedric Price, 'Non-Plan: An Experiment in Freedom', *New Society*, 20 March 1969.

4   Richard Sennett, *The Uses of Disorder: Personal Identity and City Life* (New York, 1970; London, 1971).

5   *ibid.*

6   Ioan Bowen Rees, *Government by Community* (London, 1971).

7   Walter Ullmann, *Principles of Government and Politics in the Middle Ages* (London, 1961, 1966).

8   Tom Paine, *The Rights of Man.* Pt II. Ch. 1.

9   Staughton Lynd, *Intellectual Origins of American Radicalism* (New York, 1968; London, 1969).

10 Prof. Colin Buchanan, reported in *The Sunday Times*, 25 September 1966.

11 Sherry R. Arnstein, 'A Ladder of Citizen Participation in the USA', *Journal of the American Institute of Planners*, July 1969 and *Journal of the Royal Town Planning Institute*, April 1971.

Chapter VII

1   N. J. Habraken, *Supports: an Alternative to Mass Housing* (London, 1972)

2   John Turner and Robert Fichter (eds), *Freedom to Build: Dweller Control of Housing Process* (New York, 1972).

3   Barbara Ward, *Poor World Cities* (London, 1970).

4   William P. Mangin and John C. Turner, 'Benavides and the Barriada Movement' in Paul Oliver (ed.) *Shelter and Society* (London, 1969).

5   *ibid.*

6   *ibid.*

7   Colin Ward, 'The People Act', *Freedom*, Vol. 7, No. 22, 24 August 1946

8   'The Squatters in Winter', *News Chronicle*, 14 January 1947.

9   Nicolas Walter, 'The New Squatters', *Anarchy*, Vol 9, No. 102, August 1969, reprinted in Colin Ward (ed.), *A Decade of Anarchy*, (London, Freedom Press, 1987).

10 Andrew Gilmour, *The Sale of Council Houses in Oslo* (Edinburgh, 1971) For a fuller presentation of the case for tenant control see Colin Ward, 'Tenants Take Over' (*Anarchy* 83, January 1968).

Chapter VIII

1   Ian Dunn, 'Gay Liberation in Scotland', *Scottish International Review*, March 1972.

2   John Ellerby, 'The Anarchism of Alex Comfort', *Anarchy* 33, November 1963.

3   Edmund Leach, *A Runaway World* (BBC Reith Lectures, 1967).

4   Jacquetta Hawkes in *The Human Sum* (ed.) C. H. Rolph (London, 1957).

5   John Hartwell in *Kids* No. 1, September 1972.

6   Paul and Jean Ritter, *The Free Family* (London, 1959).

7   Teddy Gold, 'The Multiple Family Housing Unit', *Anarchy* 35, January 1964.

Chapter IX

1   Frank MacKinnon, *The Politics of Education* (London, 1961).

2   Lewis Mumford, *The Condition of Man* (London, 1944).

3   William Godwin, *An Enquiry Concerning Political Justice* (London, 1793).

4   Michael Bakunin, *God and the State* (New York 1916, 1970).

5   *ibid.*

6   William Godwin, The Enquirer (London, 1797).

7   'A School the Children Won't Leave', *Picture Post*, 4 November 1944. The Story of Prestolee School is told in Gerard Holmes, *The Idiot Teacher* (London, 1952).

8   *The Teacher*, 8 April 1972.

9   Paul Goodman, *Compulsory Miseducation* (New York, 1964; London 1971).

10 Gerald Brenan, *The Literature of the Spanish People* (Cambridge, 1951).

Chapter X

1   Patrick Geddes, *Cities in Evolution* (London, 1915).

2   Agnete Vestereg in Lady Allen of Hurtwood, *Adventure Playgrounds* (London, 1949).

3   See, for example, Joe Benjamin, *In Search of Adventure* (London, 1964) and Arvid Bengtsson, *Adventure Playgrounds* (London, 1972).

4   John Lagemann, 'The Yard' in Allen, *op. cit.*

5   *The Times Educational Supplement*, 1958.

6   Peter Willmott, *The Evolution of a Community* (London, 1962).

7   J. Beresford-Ellis in *Design Magazine*, June 1963.

8   Daniel Bell, *Work and Its Discontents* (New York, 1961).

9   James J. Cox in W. R. Williams (ed.) *Recreation Places* (New York, 1958).

Chapter XI

1   Anthony Crosland in *The Observer*, 5 October 1958.

2   Branko Pribicevic, *The Shop Stewards' Movement and Workers' Control 1912-1922* (Oxford, 1959).

3   Geoffrey Ostergaard, 'Approaches to Industrial Democracy', *Anarchy* 2, April 1961.

4   Seymour Melman, *Decision-Making and Productivity* (Oxford, 1968).

5   Reg Wright, 'The Gang System in Coventry' *Anarchy* 2, April 1961, reprinted in Colin Ward (ed.), *A Decade of Anarchy*, (London, Freedom Press, 1987).

6   David Douglass, *Pit Life in Durham* (Oxford, 1972).

7   P. G. Herbst, *Autonomous Group Functioning* (London, 1962).

8   Trist, Higgin, Murray and Pollock, *Organisational Choice* (London, 1963).

9   Herbst, *op.cit.*

10 Keith Paton, 'Work and Suplus', *Anarchy* 118, 1970, reprinted in Colin Ward (ed.), *A Decade of Anarchy*, (London, Freedom Press, 1987).

11 *ibid.* Keith Paton's redeployment of the car factory is reprinted in Colin Ward, *Work* (Harmondsworth, 1972).

12 Paul and Percival Goodman, *Communitas* (Chicago, 1947).

13 Ferdynand Zweig, *The Worker in an Affluent Society* (London, 1961).

14 Keith Paton, *The Right to Work or the Fight to Live?* (Stoke-on-Trent, 1972).

Chapter XII

1   Peter Kropotkin, *The State: Its Historic Role* (London, Freedom Press, 1987).
2   Richard Titmuss, 'War and Social Policy' in his *Essays on 'The Welfare State'* (London, 1958).
3   *ibid.*
4   C. F. Masterman quoted by Heather Woolmer, 'Within the Fringe', *Town and Country Planning*, June 1972.
5   *ibid.*
6   John Bowlby, *Maternal Care and Mental Health* (London, 1952).
7   Ashley Montagu, *The Direction of Human Development* (London, 1957).
8   *The Lancet*, 22 April 1961.
9   *The Times*, 24 February 1960.
10   Norman Morris at Royal Society of Health Congress, 29 April 1961.
11   Bowlby, *op.cit.* See also Kings, Raynes and Tizard, *Patterns of Residential Care* (London, 1972).
12   Iowa Child Research Station, 1938.
13   Dorothy Burlingham and Anna Freud, *Infants Without Families* (London, 1944).
14   Margaret Neville Hill, *An Aproach to Old Age and its Problems* (London, 1960).
15   Peter Kropotkin, *Prisons and their Moral Influence on Prisoners* (1887) reprinted in Baldwin (ed.), *Kropotkin's Revolutionary Pamphlets* (New York, 1927, 1968).
16   J. B. Martin, *A Pane of Glass* (London 1960).
17   Hilliard and Munday, 'Diagnostic Problems in the Feeble-Minded', *The Lancet* (25 September 1954).
18   Dr Wadsworth, Medical Superintendent at Cheadle Royal Hospital.
19   PEP, *Community Mental Health Services* (London, 1960).
20   Dr Joshua Bierer at the 1960 conference of the World Federation of Mental Health.
21   William Godwin, *An Enquiry Concerning Political Justice* (London, 1793).
22   Kropotkin, *op.cit.*
23   Bruno Bettelheim, *The Informed Heart* (London, 1970).
24   *ibid.*
25   Russell Barton, *Institutional Neurosis* (Bristol, 1959).
26   Fenner Brockway (with Stephen Hobhouse), *English Prisons Today* (London, 1921).
27   Richard Titmuss, ('The Hospital and Its Patients' in his *Essays on 'The Welfare State'* (London, 1958).
28   John Vaizey, *Scenes from Institutional Life* (London, 1959).
29   H. von Hentig, *The Criminal and His Victim* (Yale, 1948).
30   Brian Abel-Smith, 'Whose Welfare State?' in *Conviction* (London 1958).

31 RAP, *The Case for Radical Alternatives to Prison* (London, 1971).

32 Tony Gould and Joe Kenyon, *Stories from the Dole Queue* (London, 1972).

33 Anna Coote, 'The new Aggro at the Social Security Office', *Evening Standard,* 17 April 1972.

Chapter XIII

1   H. P. Fairchild, *Dictionary of Sociology* (London, 1959).

2   William Godwin, *An Enquiry Concerning Political Justice* (London, 1793).

3   Peter Kropotkin, *Prisons and their Moral Influence on Prisoners,* 1877, reprinted in Baldwin (ed.) *Kropotkin's Revolutionary Pamphlets* (New York 1927, 1968).

4   T. B. Bottomore, *Sociology* (London, 1962).

5   Ogburn and Nimkoff, *A Handbook of Sociology* (London, 1953).

6   Jane Jacobs, *The Death and Life of Great American Cities* (London, 1961).

7   *ibid.*

8   Vernon Richards (ed.), *Errico Malatesta: His Life and Ideas* (London, Freedom Press, 1965).

9   Paul Reiwald, *Society and Its Criminals* (London, 1949).

10 Ruth S. Eissler in *Searchlights on Delinquency* (London, 1949).

Chapter XIV

1   Alexander Herzen, *From the Other Shore* (London, 1956).

2   Kenneth Burke, 'Recipe for Prosperity', *The Nation,* 8 September 1956.

3   'Blueprint for Survival', *The Ecologist,* January 1972.

4   William Morris, *News from Nowhere* (London, 1892).

5   Lewis Mumford, Introduction to the post-war edition of Ebenezer Howard, *Garden Cities of Tomorrow* (London, 1945).

6   Peter Kropotkin, *Fields, Factories and Workshops Tomorrow*, ed. by Colin Ward (London, Freedom Press, 1985).

7   'Blueprint for Survival', *The Ecologist,* January 1972.

8   George Orwell in *Poetry Quarterly,* Autumn 1945.

9   See Colin Ward, 'Harnessing the Sun', *Freedom,* 23 March 1957; 'Harnessing the Wind', *Freedom,* 13 July 1957; 'Power from the Sea', *Freedom,* 1 March 1958; Lewis Herber, 'Ecology and Revolutionary Thought', *Anarchy* 69, November 1966; 'Towards a Liberatory Technology', *Anarchy* 78, August 1967 – both the latter are reprinted in Murray Bookchin, *Post-Scarcity Anarchism* (Berkeley, Cal. 1971). See also Victor Papanek, *Design for the Real World* (London, 1972).

10 Peter Kropotkin, *op.cit.*

11 Paul Goodman, *Little Prayers and Finite Experiences* (New York, 1972).